AF371331

Mary Ann Unger

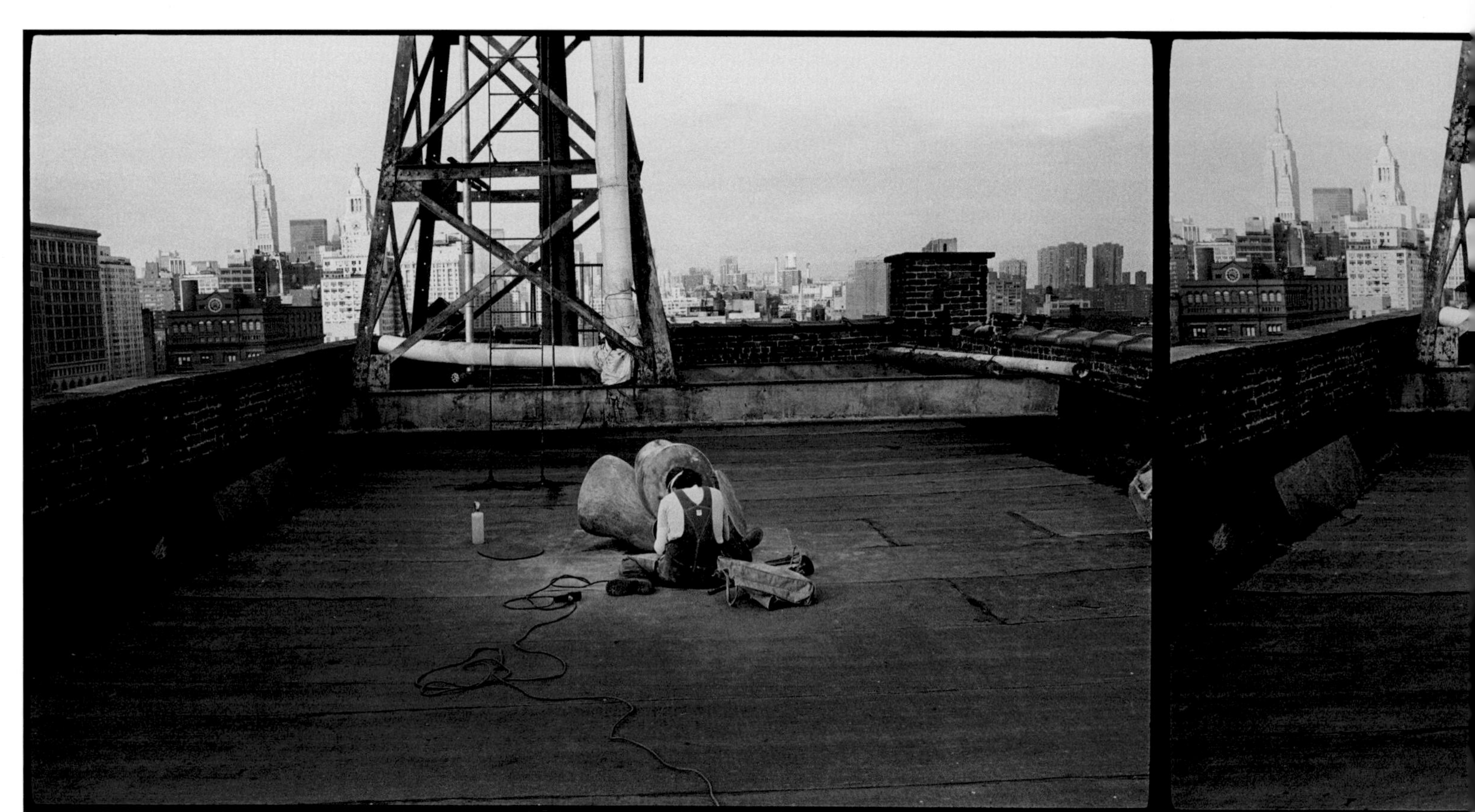

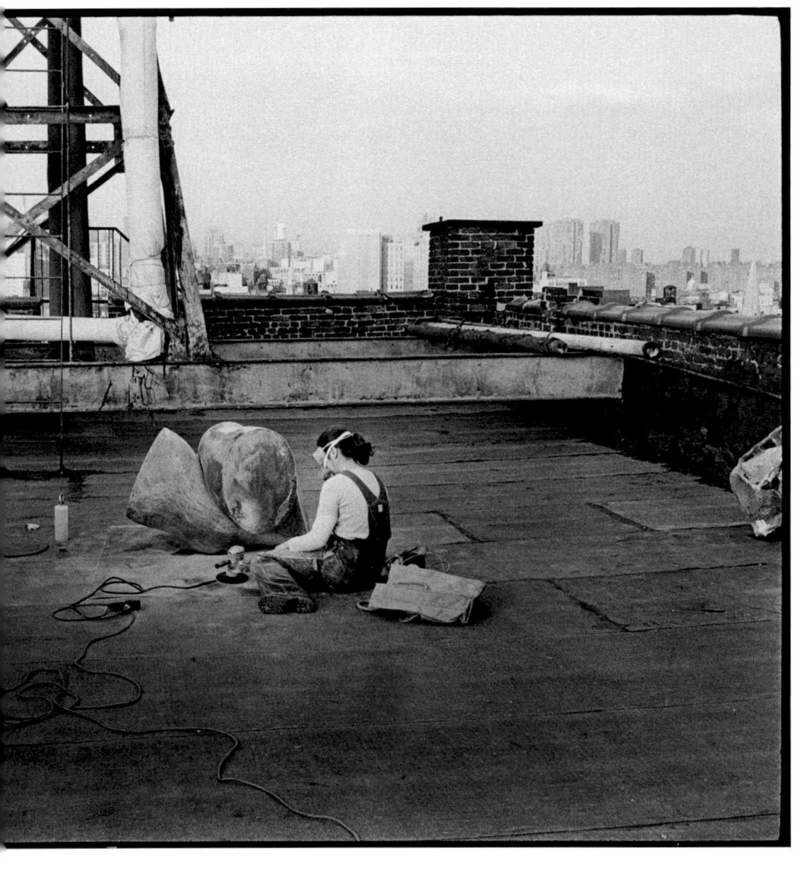

To Shape a Moon from Bone

Mary Ann Unger

Edited by Horace D. Ballard

With contributions by
Eve Biddle, Zoe Dobuler, and
Sarah Montross

Williams College Museum of Art
Williamstown, Massachusetts

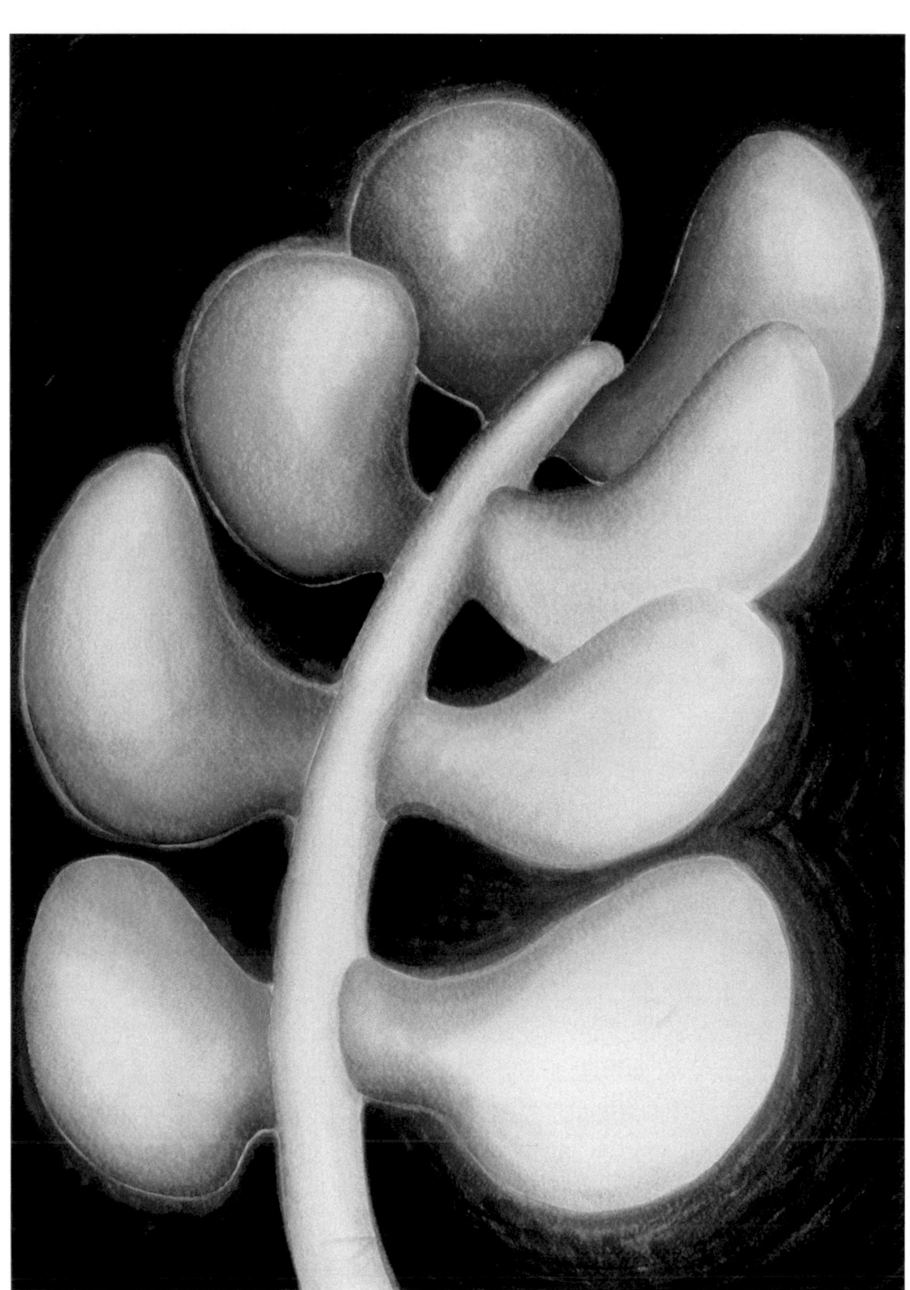

Contents

Dear S—
I've said this all before
and anyway, you had
already been picked up,
held down, put under,
and refashioned;
you were already
dreaming your body
in some gravity-less
country, already calling
it a river,…

Sister, take my hand?

Dear M—
…Unclasped
by bodies and their weight,
we start again, we take
another shape, we learn
our worth by learning
what we're not, like new
animals or children who,
finding themselves wingless, still
test the air and fall.

Dear S—
Look, there, our dead
and heavy elements
are piled high beside
the silhouette of what
we were before—look,
there our prior selves
hush out like matches
once they've lit the pyre….

Dear M—
I'd like to think as we lift
ourselves to go, in this newness
we leave it all behind—a grave, a name,
a birthday, a face—in favor
of what we know is ours
to make, this record
of our speech, our grief,
that we'll turn away from
all the doors that wouldn't
open, every collapsed bridge,
and hail instead the space
between us, shapeless and
endless as it is, though
we hold it between us
just the same.

—Molly McCully Brown and Susannah
Nevison, excerpts of epistolary exchange and
a friendship through poem

Director's Foreword

Mary Ann Unger: To Shape a Moon from Bone is a fulsome reconsideration of the multidisciplinary practice of one of the twentieth century's great artists. The posthumous survey exhibition and its attendant catalogue revive critical and scholarly attention to Unger's life and works. The project builds upon the Williams College Museum of Art's decades-old commitment to the work of female artists, curators, and scholars. With *To Shape a Moon from Bone*, we join the timely investigation undertaken by so many art museums in our cultural moment to expand the legacies of Minimalism and the archives of early conceptual art practice to include women, rigorously building out the vast network of institutions, artists, and ideas that pervaded the New York art scene in the postwar period.

Originally, this show was to be one of a pair of exhibitions on view during the 2020–21 academic year, coinciding with the yearlong celebration of fifty years of coeducation at Williams College. The pandemic-driven move to remote learning and the museum's closure to the public delayed these plans. This extended time for writing and reflection allowed organizing curator Horace D. Ballard the opportunity to expand the breadth and critical underpinnings of this volume. The result is the first scholarly positioning of Mary Ann Unger within the cultural milieu of her time. Beginning with her studies with Leo and Sandie DeLonga at Mount Holyoke College, this publication traces Unger's life, travels, and training as well as her inspirations and her extensive network of artist friends and mentors.

True to WCMA's mission of creating and inspiring exceptional experiences with art that are integral to a liberal arts education, lifelong learning, and human connection, the exhibition brings together works from the museum's holdings of African, Asian, and Pre-Columbian art with over sixty works from the Mary Ann Unger Estate to thoroughly interrogate the timely issues of lineage, influence, appropriation, and material evidence endemic to contemporary sculptural practice. The exhibition and publication offer the first curatorial assessment of the various phases and investigations Unger undertook over the entirety of her practice, amplifying specific works as culminating examples of her material experimentation. An essay by Zoe Dobuler MA '21, provides groundbreaking interpretations of Unger's monumental installation *Across the Bering Strait* (1992–94) through the lens of science fiction and feminist discourses of prehistoric migration. Opening two years later than originally slated, the exhibition changed and grew as our worldviews changed and grew. The timing could not be more perfect to bring the art world's attention to our corner of the Berkshires.

We are honored to partner with the Davidson Gallery and the Mary Ann Unger Estate to present Unger's first solo museum exhibition in more than twenty years. Max Davidson III and his son Charles, as well as Mary Ann Unger's daughter, Eve Biddle, and her husband, Josh Frankel, are all Williams alumni. Their collective support and excitement for this project is nothing short of remarkable. We are also honored that Eve has graciously loaned examples of her own exemplary art practice, extending Unger's legacy into our own moment.

Internal support at WCMA for this important exhibition has remained strong since Horace's initial spark of an idea. The logistics of installing and transporting Unger's scalar visions take diligence and creativity, and WCMA's Collections team of preparators and registrars has been exceptional. This is the kind of project we love, where each of us has a stake in the process, and I am grateful to our Communications, Engagement, Security, and Visitor Services teams who think so deeply and carefully about our various audiences engaging with Unger's legacy, both in the gallery and through virtual thresholds.

One of the joys that sometimes arise from working so closely on a survey exhibition in partnership with an artist's estate and gallery is the opportunity to make an acquisition that has transformative power for the collection. In conversation with the artist's family, Horace determined that Unger's *Shanks* (1996–97) should have a permanent home at Williams. It was the first of Unger's works that Horace saw during a visit to the estate in March 2018 and, as the following essays detail, inaugurated an incredible four-year conversation. WCMA is proud to unveil *Shanks* to our public within this exhibition.

Pamela Franks, Class of 1956 Director
Williams College Museum of Art

Director's Foreword

In 2008, the Mary Ann Unger Estate was founded with a mission that remains unchanged: to further the visibility and placement of Mary Ann Unger's work in public and private collections. The photographer Geoffrey Biddle, Mary Ann's widower, envisioned and established the Mary Ann Unger Estate with an exceptional commitment to the artist's work and drive. He is the motivator and founder of this endeavor. Our goal is to extend Mary Ann's formidable career trajectory, cut short by illness and death, and to amplify and tend to her legacy. Now, in 2022, we find ourselves fourteen years into a journey that has been profound, rewarding, and full of growth.

I have acted as the director of the estate since its founding and feel an immense sense of pride in our accomplishments. As a photographer and video artist, I am in awe of Mary Ann Unger's skill with such a wide variety of materials, her prolific output, and the fragility and strength manifest in her work. Our endeavor would not be possible without the involvement of Mary Ann and Geoffrey's daughter, Eve Biddle, an artist and cofounder of the Wassaic Project. She is a tireless fountain of energy, creative ideas, hard work, and support for both her parents' work.

Since 2011, the estate has worked with the Davidson Gallery to introduce Mary Ann's work to broader publics, one step at a time. We have brought curators, art collectors, and gallerists to her former studio space to share her life's work, her stories, her struggles, and achievements. We have showcased her work in gallery exhibitions and art fairs. We have slowly planted seeds—seeds that sometimes take years to come to fruition. As we ourselves are so taken by Mary Ann's imposing yet vulnerable work, we have been encouraged and moved by seeing the effect it continues to have on others.

Locating a curatorial partner and champion in Horace Ballard is the ultimate reward. An eloquent, sensitive, lyrical, and thoughtful curator, Horace has dedicated over four years of scholarship to understanding Mary Ann's oeuvre more deeply since Eve first introduced him to her mother's work. Horace's vision and essays bring Mary Ann, her work, and the time period in which she made it to life. They also contextualize the work, now over forty years later, and illuminate elements of it that are both constant and changing. We are so grateful to Horace for recognizing the power of Mary Ann's work to resonate with and captivate others.

That the Williams College Museum of Art (WCMA) is organizing the first solo museum exhibition of Mary Ann Unger's work in over twenty years poetically links together many threads of her life. The artist's connections to western Massachusetts abound: Mary Ann was an alumna of Mount Holyoke College, while Eve attended Williams College, as did several members of the Davidson family. This exhibition of Mary Ann's sculpture and works on paper, which also includes works by her daughter, brings a lifetime of work and family full circle for Mary Ann Unger and Eve Biddle.

We hope that this long-awaited survey of Mary Ann's career, along with the acquisition of *Shanks* (1996–97) by WCMA, will continue to enhance the visibility of her work. For others to see her skill with materials, her joy and pain in her lived experience, her wrestling with questions of life and death, big and small, everyday and spiritual. For the work to be shared. For her legacy to grow. For her practice to be in the minds of future makers.

We are so grateful to Horace Ballard, Lisa Dorin, Pamela Franks, and all the staff and supporters at WCMA for championing Mary Ann Unger's work and making this exhibition and acquisition possible.

Allison Kaufman, Director
Mary Ann Unger Estate

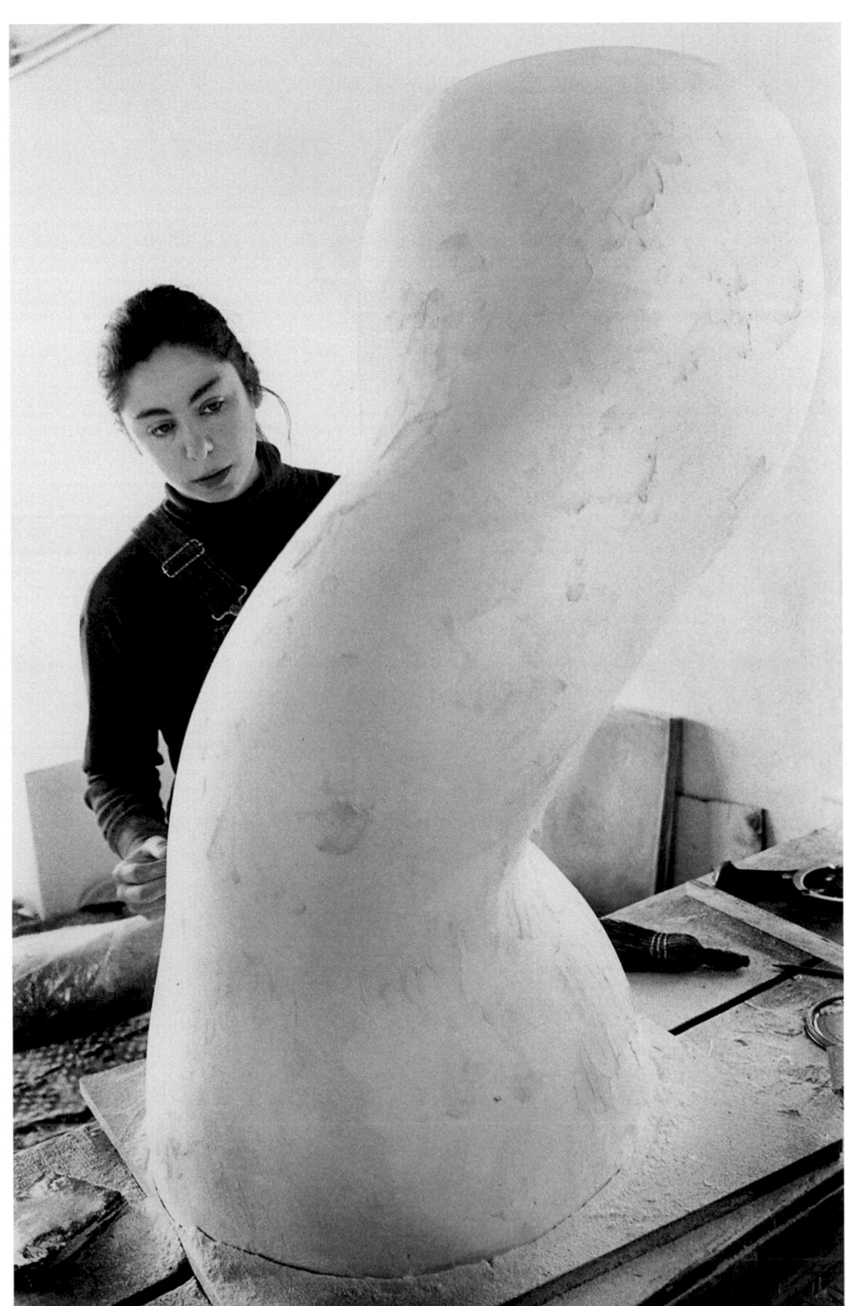

Mary Ann Unger
Influences and Arrangements

Horace D. Ballard

The forging of an art practice is a life's work. Mary Ann Unger (fig. 1.1) sought connection and synergies across cultures, places, and peoples; her work emerged "out of encounter."[1] In her practice, oblong, mycorrhizal arrangements permit an emotive experience beyond language. Modeled dimensional forms draw viewers into encounters with space, with one another, and with themselves. The values of connection and encounter that propelled Unger's life are inextricable from the attentions and pursuits of her practice. In this sense, Unger tapped into the animating force of sculpture's immediacy: its mimetic sense of life, the medium's dimensionality a map of the living pulse that gave it shape. This essay explores Unger's life—its broad contours within history and her aesthetic influences—to reveal, by default, life's extensions into the work.

In Unger's hand, the formal elements of art function as poetic susurrus rather than as strictures or responses that need to be mastered, reduced, and refined in construction. Unger sculpts as if she is composing texts, in which meaning supersedes or suffuses the surface of form. This tendency—to flood the line, to extend the eye, to expand a viewer's self-awareness of their own movements in space—has been called many things. Given Unger's demonstrable skill in pattern making and graphic design, I have termed this quality "expressive typography" and use it throughout this essay in effort to blur the distinctions between the handiwork of written expression and sculpted expression. By collecting Unger's various preoccupations under this phrase, I also hope to capture the artist's intent to convey to the viewer the individual and collective experience of pain, love, enchantment, and wonder with life and with history, even in the face of death, without over-determining the meaning of a work or its interpretation.

Influences
Early Years | 1945–1972

Mary Ann Unger was born in New York City in 1945. She came of age in the New Jersey suburbs of Bergen County and the streets of Manhattan in the decades following the Second World War.[2] A regular visitor to the museums along Fifth Avenue, Unger took classes at the Museum of Modern Art, where she frequently modeled animals and human figures in clay. When she asked her parents if it was possible for a woman to become a sculptor, they replied, "Yes, Louise Nevelson was."[3]

Unger attended Mount Holyoke College, enrolling in the fall of 1963. Coming from "three generations of engineers" in the "era of Sputnik," Unger initially set aside her love for modeling form and focused on courses

Mary Ann Unger working in her studio, Third Street, New York, 1980. Photo by Geoffrey Biddle. Courtesy of the artist.

"

that would lead to a degree in biochemistry.[4] But after "a year of broken test tubes,"[5] she changed her major and received a bachelor's degree in art in 1967.

Mount Holyoke hired Leonard "Leo" DeLonga (1925–1991) to start the sculpture program during Unger's first year. A gifted and charismatic mentor with a background working in the Pittsburgh steel mills, he was a multidisciplinary artist influenced by the fluid surrealism of Jean Arp and Max Ernst. DeLonga made the basement of his home the college's sculpture studio in the early years, and students came over for breakfast and then stayed for class. It was here Unger "learned to weld, cast bronze, and carve marble."[6] DeLonga conducted his studio as "a laboratory of curiosity" and taught young sculptors, as one former student noted, a "practical approach to the physics and chemistry of metallurgy."[7] Students in advanced classes were treated to the joint tutelage of DeLonga and his partner, the noted ceramist Sandra "Sandie" DeLonga (born 1929). It is probable that many of the sculptural students of the period became adept at working in clay and slip, plaster, cement, and lightweight industrial-grade Hydrocal through Sandie DeLonga.[8]

During the 1960s and 1970s, Leo DeLonga was best known for large-scale, welded-metal forms in steel and bronze that functioned as a kind of high modern and geometric rejoinder to medieval tapestries. His aesthetic sensibility was animated by a sense of formal dissonance: counterbalancing the intellectual "heft" of a subject with materials that might seem incongruous in order to capture a sense of cosmic equilibrium and/or levity. For example, in DeLonga's *Warriors* (1962), two armies of two dozen warriors in the throes of battle are carved out of an 8 × 22 × 8–inch block of alabaster. In an untitled work from the mid-1970s, the mythic apparition of Zeus to Danae as an ephemeral golden mist of rain and twinkling light is translated into a solid bronze altarpiece with two six-foot paneled doors of cast and welded bronze, which fold close and hinge open to reveal a field of burnished copper and bronze shingles.[9]

Twenty years after she began studio work with the DeLongas, Unger recalled that "Michelangelo, Rodin, Henry Moore, and Giacometti were [her] heroes"[10] during college. It was in her sophomore and junior years that she began to scrutinize images of their work to parse out the paths around certain intentions she would negotiate for the remainder of her practice, including the centrality of the human figure; the mediation of language and visual metaphor; sign and signification; and the balance of interior, exterior, and anterior spaces. But of the many lessons Unger took from the DeLongas, chief among them was the revelation that sculpture is not a fixed category of making. It is, rather, a language full of spatial and material possibility. And the wealth of possibilities of expression in three dimensions gave the young artist permission to experiment and build her own relationship to ephemeral experience and its tangible augmentations through an idea of modular forms that could be fabricated at scale and arranged, like arranging type. Unger also gleaned how the rhythmic and lyrical dialectics or interplays possible within the language of sculpture, that is, between mass and scale, or between color and abstraction, offered dissonant relationships that took time to resolve, lengthening the moment of coexistence, encounter, and empathy between the hand of the sculptor and the viewer.

Joining Unger among the DeLongas' students in these years were the artist and future museum director Elizabeth Egbert (1945–2014) and artist, future gallerist, and inventor Susan Mohl Powers (born 1944), whose career still encompasses sculpture and installation, incorporating planar and polygon-shaped metal assemblages, painting, and sewn fabric. Egbert and Unger remained close friends throughout their lives.

Outside and inside the studio, the world turned. Unger and her peers came to an understanding of themselves as artists in one of the most charged moments in the critical trajectories of academic thought as well as in US history. The Neo-Dada and Pop Art revolutions that were buoyant during the mid to late 1960s balked at de Saussurian structuralism and interpretation. Instead, they embraced the Derridian revival of the Platonic question "Can a thing be both 'the thing' and a symbol of the thing?" or "Must a thing be just 'the thing,' or can it be a symbol of what possessing that thing conveys?" that would galvanize deconstructionist theory. But one's intellectual life was understood as sutured to one's political consciousness. And the period was suffused with televised actions of activism and grief. The March on Washington for Jobs and Freedom would have occurred just weeks before Unger matriculated. The Reverend Dr. Martin Luther King Jr. spoke at Mount Holyoke's Gettell Amphitheater on October 20, 1963, a month into her first year of college (fig. 1.2). John F. Kennedy was assassinated just a month later, the Dallas incident just days before her first Thanksgiving break. The succeeding two-year period of popular and political spectacles broadcast through television—the Kennedy funeral, the signing of the Civil Rights Act of 1964, the signing of the Voting Rights Act of 1965— provided iconic cultural and political moments that defined citizenship and early Pop Art aesthetics.

In this fluctuating, violent, and heady milieu, Unger and her contemporaries began "to quietly contend with the ways in which structures of power invade the most intimate spaces of the self."[11] In her seminars in history, anthropology, art history, and literature, Unger recognized that the relationship between language and feeling, and between language and signs and significations, proves oddly visual in its connotative textures and patternings. One wonders if she found joy in the positioning of visible and auditory convergence at the heart of Derridian deconstruction and postwar literary studies. In the studio, in late-night conversations, in the headlines, and on the stage of the lecture hall during panels and lyceum speeches, Unger would have been attuned to the language with which bright minds of her generation were leveraging abstraction and critical theory as

tools to be directed and employed on any subject, from the malignments of the male gaze to political disaffection with the US role in wars around the world. This transitive thinking comes through in Unger's mind, even years later, in 1994, as she riffs during an artist's talk, "As one gets further away from an experience, I think one is better able to communicate, to signify something.... That's kind of strange about communication and visual abstraction."[12]

The relationship between language and truth and the politics of the personal has further consequence at this moment in Unger's formation when we look at the slate of honorary degree recipients and commencement speakers for her graduating class in 1967. We cannot know if Unger viewed any of these individuals as personal sheroes, or if Unger remembered their remarks years later. But their shared presence and their words during Senior Week and the traditions of Canoe Sing, the final lecture, and the parade through the Field Gate would have been moments of heightened attention: these were the voices her peers and her faculty felt could best provide the perspectives needed to sum up the college experience, as well as the guidance desired to build a bridge to the new chapters to come. With the largest number of recipients since the war, honorary degrees that year went to Katherine Graham, editor and publisher of the *Washington Post*; Hedley Donovan, editor of the *New York Times*; poet and anti-war activist Robert McCloskey; Louise Hall Tharp, the historian and recent biographer of the American sculptor Augustus Saint-Gaudens and the life and art passions of Isabella Stewart Gardner; and Anna Mary Wells, Mount Holyoke Class of 1926, who was the faculty and student choice for that year's alumni award for her multidisciplinary practice as a writer of biography, essays, fiction, and poetry.[13]

In 1967, Unger moved to Berkeley, California, and elected studio courses at the University of California. She took three courses: sculptural assemblage with Robert "Bob" Hudson (born 1938); geometric abstraction in painting and ceramics with Jim Melchert (born 1930); and expressionist ceramics from Peter Voulkos

1.2
The Reverend Dr. Martin Luther King Jr. speaking in Gettell Amphitheater at Mount Holyoke College, October 20, 1963. Courtesy of MHC Archives / Vincent S. D'Addario.

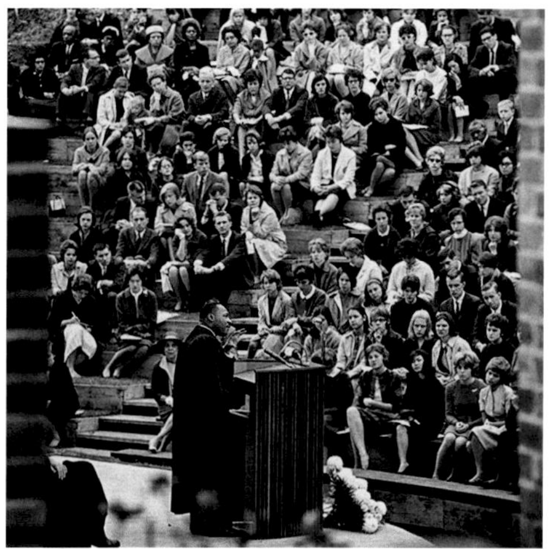

(1924–2002)—the latter having recently founded the ceramics departments at Otis College in 1954 and at UC Berkeley in 1959 (now the Program of Art and Design).[14]

The year in Berkeley is a "silent" period of Unger's development in the written archives, but silence is not *absence*. As Barbara Hepworth reminds us, *presence* and active meanings "emerge more powerfully when they are carried through a sculptor's own silent language."[15] And what is this silent language? It is the visible sign of the times she navigated and breathed into. Unger was in Berkeley in the spring of 1968 during the assassinations of King and, a few months later, Robert F. Kennedy. These events spurred the incorporation and public actions of the Black Panther Party in nearby Oakland the same year.

Reflecting on her time at Berkeley two decades later, Unger wrote that she was involved in the coalition-driven free-speech and anti-war movements at the time. We should recall that these student-led movements at Berkeley transfixed and galvanized the nation (fig. 1.3). The free-speech and anti-war demonstrations also brought together students and community members from the Bay Area who would form satellite groups agitating for equity and self-determination based on gender and race.[16] (These demonstrations and actions led to the creation of the university's Department of Ethnic Studies in 1971.) While we do not know exactly in which actions and which demonstrations and protests and sit-ins and learn-ins and be-ins Unger participated, we know that she was in Berkeley at the moment of critical juncture between second- and third-wave feminist interrogations around what we now term intersectional identities.

Unger's time in Berkeley was rich and layered and remained culturally relevant to the ideas and aesthetic attentions that contoured her practice for the next twenty years. In addition to the music, and the sights, sounds, sweat, smells, and colors of Berkeley and the light off the hills of the East Bay,

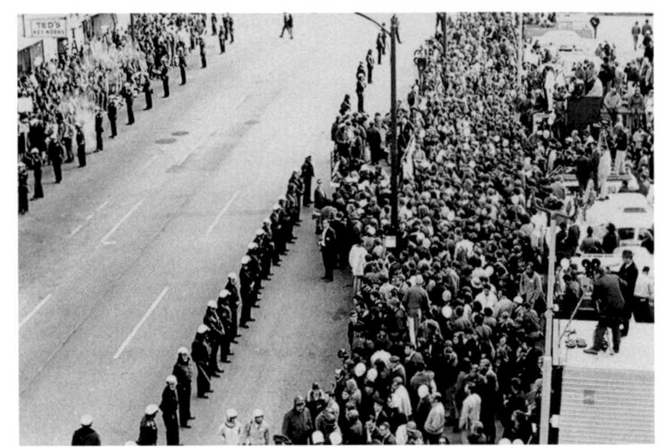

1.3
Free speech protest, Berkeley, California, c. 1967–68. Courtesy of the Archives of the *Daily Californian*, University of California, Berkeley.

Unger would have seen flyers for the Rainbow Sign and womxn's bars along Solano Street. These establishments not only gave womxn spaces to gather, socialize, and strategize, but also gave womxn artists of all genres and intersectional identities places to show or make work in community.[17] This year in the Bay Area provided Unger with a cosmopolitan and politically charged immersion in the critical vocabularies of comparative and ecumenical humanism. A deep takeaway was the sense that language, especially political rhetoric, no matter how inclusive, cannot change culture alone. Though a word is an object, and though language is an act, verbal and written expressions require actualization in the mode of visible and tangible forms of policy, infrastructure, monument, and representational politics—to embed meaning. And what is meaning but viewer, space, and place in "personal integration"?[18] This factor is the key formal technique to "developing the poetry which is [the sculptor's] free and affirmative contribution to society."[19]

One can imagine Unger in these years performing what Rosalind Krauss terms "perpetual inventory":[20] tallying up, measuring, sorting, identifying, discarding, holding up multiple facets of herself, from her North Jersey–Manhattan roots to her education and travels, to her identities as a woman, as a Jew, as a maker with ambition. Third-world and third-wave feminist and womanist collectives in the Bay Area and Southern California were pointing to the assumptions made and exclusions of Euro-American feminisms of the first and second waves. Unger would have been spurred to reflect on her privilege

Ballard

and on the myriad constructions and performances of femininity and womanhood that she saw, experienced, and navigated. Famously, Krauss's articulation is paired with a sense of postmodern farewell—the sense that after high modernism, authorial intent and conception matter more than the choice of medium (and the possibilities and limits) leveraged. The fulsome connotations of the phrase "perpetual inventory" seem to fit Unger well.

In the fall of 1968, Unger returned to New York, but not for long. The next three and a half years were a prolonged season of odd jobs and international travel, of which Unger writes, "My artistic horizons were wrenched open and I was cut loose to drift."[21] She embarked during this period on her own kind of "grand tour" and traveled widely—sometimes with a companion but often solo—collecting experiences and objects with tactile and immediate material potency. Crossing and recrossing the border into Mexico. Traveling to Switzerland, where she linked up with a group of young artists interested in "environmental happenings." A trek to Nepal that yielded hammered-tin kitchen utensils. A treasured, bespoke caftan made for her in Morocco that attested to herculean stories of when she crossed a portion of the Sahara alone in a van. Teaching art classes in the New Mexico desert. Returning to the Sahara, where, on a third trip across, she was accosted by a group of young men who wanted her and her fire and her provisions, and safely survived. Then there was the time she crossed into Côte d'Ivoire on a commercial freighter, the only passenger, the only non-African, and the only woman aboard.

Travel and the "relationship between figure and landscape is vitally important for the sculptor," Barbara Hepworth wrote a generation before, as it "opens up an infinite variety of continuous curves in the third dimension."[22] The world does not form itself into boundaries. It takes the human instrument to see, to experience, to frame. The world is and the world continues, and in its continuity the world redoubles and reforms itself. One wonders if Unger began

to understand that synergy so often cast as a duality between self and other in language, but far more fluid or coeval in art. As Hepworth articulates, "There is no landscape without the human figure: it is impossible to contemplate [space and prehistory] in the abstract."[23]

These vignettes of a life, of a young woman's life, somehow seem more than experience. They read as history, as the personal praxis of a "closer connection to life and a closer, physical relationship between peoples,"[24] or the ever-fluid, nonlinear, more capacious epistemes of *historias*. This concept offers us a mode of considering the experience of simultaneously observing and intervening in place. It allows us to frame what we cannot know about her day-to-day thoughts while simultaneously drawing on the artist's later words and work to reflect upon how such a dynamic period surely informed Unger's sense of the world and sense of her own story being concomitant with history, writ large. Imagine Mary Ann Unger in the human position of flux: intrepid, curious, open, in love, and inspiring love. She had thoughts and she was delighted by things and missed other things. She remembered this period of travel as "frightening and exhilarating. I did many watercolors and laid out spiral constructions with twigs in the sand—*Spiral Jetty* was on my mind."[25]

We can imagine her doing what artists do: reading, sketching, making notes about materials to source when back in the States; writing broken words that are and are not poetry, trying to circle in on the nut, the core of meaning; trying to remember and refine a key phrase from a lecture, or the translation of a word from one language to another that reconciles a textbook definition with the actual artifact and ritual in front of one's face. We can feel her finding joy in unexpected solace, and the mix of frustration and wonder that comes with immersion in a new space that is always unfolding and that demands one's continual sense of present-ness and attention, for safety, for fear you could "miss" something extraordinary. And as much as she is taking in the sounds, the smells, the feel of sweat and breeze in new places on the body, she is there to study structures: both human formed and natural, augmented, eroded, desecrated, sacred, politicized, forgotten. In so doing, she begins to piece together the aesthetic attentions of the next thirty years of her life and practice.

In 1972, Unger returned home, confident that she had "found something that was my own: repeated biomorphic shapes that grew in progression. This pulled together several aspects of my roots, and influences."[26] She had been accepted into the painting and sculpture master of fine arts cohort at Columbia University, and she was ready. The New York Unger returned to was changed and changing. She immersed herself in the developing scene of downtown galleries, loft parties, viewings, happenings, and the ever-present museum presentations that shift the art market and the discourses of art history.

Return to New York | 1972

Returning to New York in the early 1970s positioned Mary Ann Unger on the track toward the work we know today: the con-struction and orchestration of oblique, tensile elements—on paper and in volumic form. It was in this chapter of her life that Unger began making shapes and structures that, while engaged with the academic qualities of scale, color, proportion, and positive/negative space, were also provoca-tions toward new and expanded orientations of relationship between the viewer and the object, between the eye and the desire to touch.

In her description of the primacy of the direct and discursive line as the formal hinge in three dimensions that "interlocks and interweaves… allowing the artist to go anywhere,"[27] Ruth Asawa articulated the kinds of radical reconsiderations of planar geometries and the function of asymmetries that were giving initial shape to postmodern explorations of conceptual expression at that moment. The divergent collateral of the line gave permission for the art scene to embark on a wholesale spatial inquiry, in which Unger invested deeply. Throughout her

graduate studies at Columbia, the language of indeterminacy, affect, and intuitive gesture was permeating New York as alumni of Black Mountain College began to take leading positions as faculty and curators at art institutions in the city. Their influence honed students' attentions to the distinctions between self-disclosure and expression, while eliding the perceived separation between the intellectual working out of challenges (impositions) in three dimensions and the intuitive response of the sketch or study.

In studio and in "crit"; in museum galleries and at the bar afterward, discussing what was on view and how curators attended (or failed to attend) to artist intentions; in conversation with her studio and art history faculty—Kurt Varnedoe and Meyer Shapiro were still teaching then—and her peers, such as Helene Brandt, Vincent Ciniglio (who remained a close friend), Edward Kimball, Sylvia Netzer (Unger's best friend), Helene Pardee, Don Porcaro, Ursula von Rydingsvard, and Joan Weber, Unger began to pay close attention to the edges and spaces between elements, and how the zones of jointing, whether notched, resting, or held together, could be leveraged to emotional effect. The history of art faculty would have joined their studio colleagues in a deep interroga-tion of how materials and surfaces preface volume—and how confrontational and interventionist installation design could elicit affective responses in the viewer.[28]

During Unger's three years as a student in Columbia's MFA cohort, the New York art scene offered dialectic approaches to sculpture and the political and cultural response of the medium to "the end of modernism." The galleries, such as Paula Cooper (the first of the SoHo galleries, fig. 1.4), 112 Greene Street, Artist Restaurant, and nearly eighty others, were pivoting to varying degrees toward what we would now term conceptual and performance-based practices and presentations. Congregated around SoHo and, increasingly, Chelsea, the downtown gallery scene aimed to bring the lifeblood of a rapidly gentrifying and shrinking city into the art space, leveraging artist-run spaces and cooperatives in the

Ballard

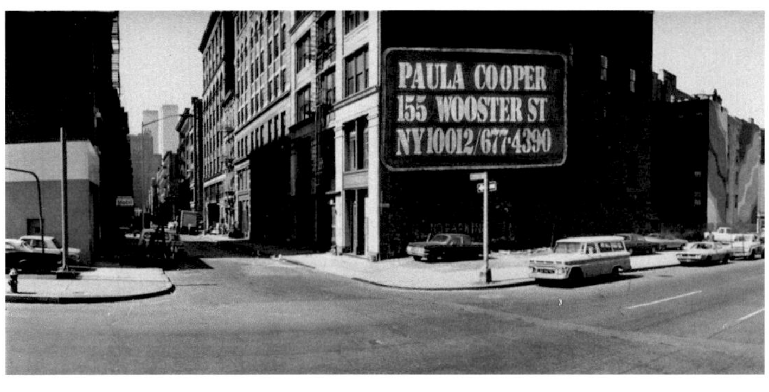

1.4
The Paula Cooper Gallery, second location, at 155 Wooster Street, in SoHo, New York, 1973. Photo by Mates and Katz. Courtesy of the Paula Cooper Gallery.

1.5
Installation view of Nathan Rabin, *Lynda Benglis: Sparkle Knots*, in the *Clocktower* exhibition at PS1, December 6, 1973– January 19, 1974. Museum of Modern Art Archives, New York, INPS1.14.1.

neighbor-hoods where artists lived as nodes of culture and gathering— as places where different kinds of art at different scales were juxtaposed together or shown consecutively with little fanfare. They were places where "happenings" happened. Carl Andre, Lynda Benglis, Trisha Brown, Dan Flavin, Joan Jonas, Donald Judd, Joseph Kosuth, Sol LeWitt (offering the first wall drawings), Robert Mangold, Bruce Nauman, and Robert Ryman showed alongside Jasper Johns, Ed Ruscha, Cy Twombly, and Andy Warhol.

From the postwar period into the 1980s, the aspirational artist's trajectory solidified as progressing from an MFA program to gallery representation, to successive group shows and critical attention, to a museum presentation and a review in "the *Times*." The midtown and uptown museums maintained the status quo of high modernism and were objects of derision, critique, and envy (much as they remain today). And yet, we must remember that folk like Andre, Jonas, and Robert Rauschenberg, as well as some of the artists associated with Fluxus experimentation, among them Joseph Beuys, Yoko Ono, and Nam June Paik, showed both uptown and downtown, sometimes concurrently. For any young artist, but particularly for a sculptor, such alignments and disparities proved heady and exciting, as well as confusing.

Mary Ann Unger seems to have thrived and taken inspiration from all of it— private gallery, artist co-op, public museum. She was a kind of museum flaneur— attending to everything and anything if there was time. Her voracious exploration of the city's galleries and museums each season continued for over twenty years. But perhaps it was a handful of now-iconic presentations at the Guggenheim, the Jewish Museum, and the Museum of Modern Art (the Modern, or MoMA) that most contoured her own considerations of material, as well as how critics would soon respond to her practice.

The Guggenheim offered Unger four now-iconic presentations during her student years: Eva Hesse's 1972 retrospective, followed by the Giacometti and Max Ernst retrospectives of 1974, and the 1974–75 *Masters of Modern Sculpture* exhibition, which installed works from the Guggenheim collections side by side with works from two famous private collections. This last exhibition may well have been the first time Unger encountered a group of Isamu Noguchi sculptures in dialogue together in one room.[29]

Unger may very well have missed the Modern's presentation of Tony Smith in the late fall / early winter of 1971 and '72. However, it is possible she would have seen (and she definitely would have heard about) the museum's project space at 10 Bleeker Street (MoMA PS1 "off site") where, during June of 1972, *5 Sculptors—7,000 Sq. Feet* featured massive wood and iron works by Cecile Abish, Bill Bollinger, Peter Gourfain, Robert Grosvenor, and Jene Highstein.[30] One also wonders if MoMA PS1's 1973–74 premiere of Lynda Benglis's *Sparkle Knots* (fig. 1.5) would have been on Unger's mind when she installed several of her own works in the same space in the 1977 exhibition *10 Downtown, 10 Years*.

In September and October of 1972, a small show at the Modern of roughly sixteen votive- and cabinet-sized sculptures from Jean Arp, Louise Bourgeois, Constantin Brancusi, Barbara Hepworth, Gabriel Kohn, Henry Moore, and three others may have been one of the first museum shows Unger and her cohort visited together—perhaps followed by beers, or lunch, and debate. *Luise Kaish: Sculpture* (fig. 1.6) at the Jewish Museum in 1973 may have been the first solo museum survey of a female sculptor, and of a female Jewish sculptor, that Mary Ann Unger

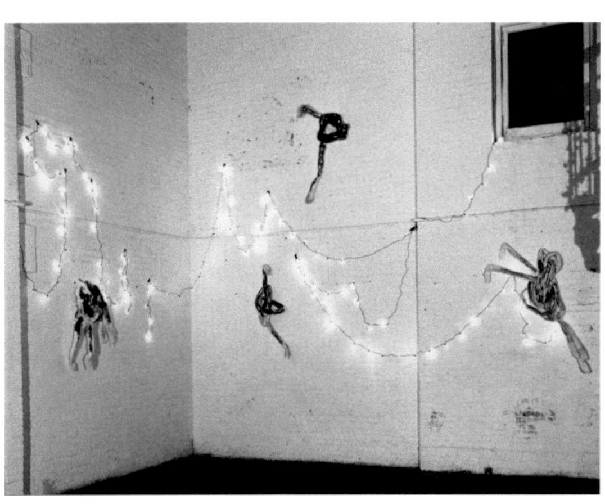

visited. Like Unger, Kaish was a New York–based artist who had traveled widely and returned to the city for a comfortable yet rigorous career. She worked in large-scale bronze sculpture and cabinet-scale forms in steel and aluminum, as well as lithography, watercolor, collage, and oil painting, garnering commissions for the city's synagogues and temples while also teaching (she would become head of Columbia's graduate program of painting and sculpture two years after Unger graduated). Kaish's multidisciplinary sensorium must have been pleasing for the young Unger, who traversed similar modalities, depending on her intentions. For her mid-career survey, the curator and scholar Avram Kampf wrote of Kaish's sculpture, "Freed from its fixed collective symbolism, these sculptures represent an inward voyage into the hidden

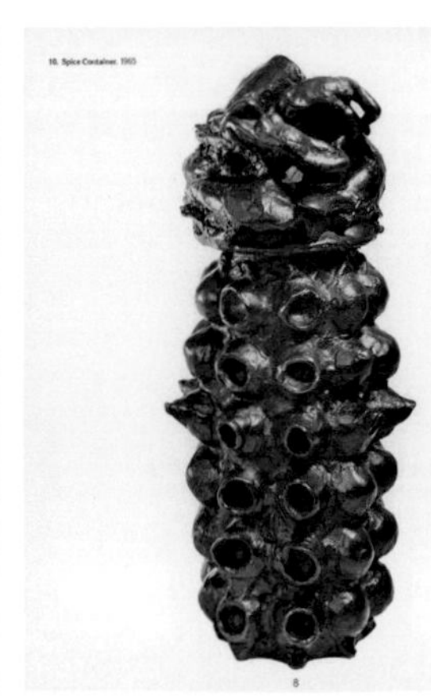

recesses of the artist's self, following its delicate and secret movements… passionate, exhilarating and 'unselfing.'… These new abstract works which supersede her early more expressive or romantic ones… place [Kaish] in the mainstream of contemporary art."[31] Similar reflections would accompany reviews of Unger's work over the course of the following two decades.[32]

This heady zeitgeist, rich in the dialectics and attentions of the art world, greeted Unger on her homecoming and would sustain her for the rest of her life. The galleries and museums of the city offered a kind of cocurricular education in sculpture's reception and the possibilities of installation within a gallery to bisect or extend architectural space. Being in New York also gave Unger permission to prod the nature of the ways in which the contemporary political contexts of one's time engage with the personal. As John Russell wrote in his review of *Jewish Experience in the Art of the Twentieth Century* (1975) at the Jewish Museum, "It would be difficult to think of a more ambitious, delicate and difficult subject…. Great themes do not always make for great art."[33] Unger had come to New York to make great art and to be a working artist in a vibrant ecosystem of artists. She had come to refine her eye and to train her hand.

Columbia | 1972–1975

The students concentrating in sculpture in Columbia's MFA cohort of 1975 were instructed and mentored by three formidable talents: Ronald Bladen, Minoru Niizuma, and George Sugarman. All three belonged (with Agnes Martin, Al Held, and Ellsworth Kelly) to a generation of artists that, as Roberta Smith expertly couches, "never quite earned a name or adopted a polemic" but "evolved an intuitive, slightly biomorphic geometric style that sidestepped the emotional gesturalism of Abstract Expressionism and… set the stage for Minimalism."[34]

Ronald Bladen (1918–1988) began lecturing at Columbia in Unger's last full year of the program, fresh from his inclusion in the 1973 Whitney Biennial, and his influence must have been considerable. The languid proportions of Bladen's economical and industrial-looking forms, with rhapsodic allusions to the European Mannerists, as well as to the postwar Constructivists, heralded a romantic turn for large-scale minimalist sculpture.[35] Bladen formed a scalar and material bridge for Unger from Arp, Ernst, and Noguchi to the work she was seeing in the downtown galleries.

Already being cited in the early seventies by Carl Andre, Donald Judd, and Sol LeWitt as a major influence, Bladen was a sought-after instructor, with good looks, Hollywood connections, and downtown credentials

Ballard

through the defunct, but no-less-legendary avant-garde Tenth Street Gallery milieu via the Brata Gallery. Bladen reveled in jumping between drawing, painting, irregular votive forms, and large-scale installation, evincing a spiritual rather than a formal continuity across his career. This seems to have resonated with DeLonga's approach and deeply influenced Unger's own manner of working between several media at once. Given his prominence and guest lectureship at Columbia, Bladen most likely oversaw Unger's thesis presentation in the spring of 1975.

George Sugarman (1912–1999) was a prolific artist and consummate teacher. Known for innovating pedestal-free sculpture and biomorphic metal sculpture in vivid colors,[36] Sugarman also saw himself as a multidisciplinary artist working across painting, drawing, and sculpture. He encouraged his students to do the same. Though his earliest sculpted forms were in wood, he shifted to metalworking in the late 1950s, making and exhibiting forms that seemed like crouching armatures waiting for the softening resolution of plaster.[37] In 1974, Sugarman was quoted as saying, "All art is metaphor.… To escape from metaphor, artists have often chosen… sheer physical stimulation or the insistence on a system of formal relationships that has meaning in and for itself. Metaphor, stimulation, formal relationships, three ways to meaning. Is it necessary to choose?"[38]

This statement, from the period when Unger was his student, provides insight into Sugarman's pedagogy. In his sculptural practice, Sugarman modeled for his students and contemporaries how to "contract the body into its most powerful synecdoche"[39] by deploying grounded, horizontal forms at scale that demand viewers spend time negotiating or changing their paths through a space. Such works force encounters between artist and viewer that provide the simulation of pure presence through the language of sculpture. Sugarman would have encouraged Unger to leverage her own body and its capacities, challenges, and emotions as a jumping-off point for the expressive impulses sculpture has always channeled for the maker and the viewer.

Sugarman's influence informed Unger's explorations of working with armatures, using a ribbed chassis or undercarriage to provide shape and support, but also to add volume and anthropoid proportions while disguising mass. At Columbia, Unger devised a particular process for constructing the large-scale outdoor works that she would continue into the early 1990s. She would first wrap a welded armature of a six- or eight-inch metal rod in chicken wire, then plaster it. Next, Unger would make a soft mold in rubber before casting the piece in tinted fiberglass or concrete.[40]

Minoru Niizuma (1930–1998) imparted two fundamental skills to his students and peers: a rigorous understanding of the properties and possibilities of working with stone, and a kind of mythic compression, where ancient and prehistoric forms and their modern variants can "compress" Neolithic myth and quotidian contemporary life, yielding potent new forms with a vast emotional expanse across cultures and geographies and time. After graduating from Tokyo University of the Arts (then, Tokyo National University of Fine Arts and Music) in 1955, Niizuma moved to New York[41] and worked between the United States, Japan, and Portugal for the remainder of his life and career. From 1964 to 1970, he was an instructor at the Art School of the Brooklyn Museum. He came to national prominence through inclusion in *The New Japanese Painting and Sculpture* (1965–77)—a seven-venue traveling exhibition organized by Dorothy C. Miller and William S. Lieberman for the Museum of Modern Art. Niizuma began adjuncting at Columbia University in 1972 and remained affiliated until 1984, when he moved to Portugal.

In the early 1980s, Niizuma founded what is now styled the North American Sculpture Center in Westbury, New York, to supply stone artists with space and materials. Working mostly at scale in marble, Niizuma was also adept at carving granite, volcanic rock, and basalt. He would sometimes put on public demonstrations of rock carving with other sculptors in the streets of New York, shutting down traffic and blurring the lines between sculpture, mass actions, academic discourse, happenings, and performance. Along with

Philip Pavia, Karl Prantl, and Paul Jenkins, Niizuma participated in the inaugural Sculpture Symposiums organized by Prantl for Cooper Hewitt's Museum of Design, "marble dust and power tools everywhere."[42]

Inspired by traditional Japanese textiles and ritual ceramics, as well as nature and prehistoric menhirs and monoliths, Niizuma shaped stone into geometric and abstracted forms resembling pelvises, whetstones, thigh bones, waves, tree bark, mold blooms, geometric tattoos, tree rings, fired-but-unglazed vessels, and pestles and mortars. Niizuma would have encouraged Unger to further her interest in sited sculpture that neither impinges upon nor changes a landscape but arises from it and somehow makes it more of what it is. Niizuma's own interrogation of surface as a formal element equivalent to mass/space, would have been instructive for Unger, building on her long-term relationship with ceramics and with the notion of burnishing and finish in her undergraduate experience with welded bronze.

Niizuma sometimes invited his students to his loft on 168th Street so that they could see how a working sculptor lived and worked in the same space. He also wanted them to immediately sense how sculpture reanimates and reconceives architectural spaces that are not the white cube of modern museums.[43]

Unger found in Niizuma's sculptural language a comparable striving toward a synthesis of modular semiotic forms that he returned to, over and over again, in various materials and scalar arrangements. His work and teaching emboldened his students to search for a new lexicon for monumental sculpture by looking to the non-Western and the prehistoric. He encouraged them to set aside hierarchies of genre and media and gather references widely in order to compress forms and resonances from several cultures into a new singularity. Such rendered forms would offer a consistent and timeless vision of what sculpture could manifest when intentionally sited in an environment.

Study at Columbia focused and refined Unger's gestures, directing her synthetic and singular modes of intercultural exchange toward specificity and decades-long investigations of materials. She learned from Bladen, Niizuma, and Sugarman how to clarify the textural language of knuckled tessellations and post-and-lintel construction that would become her formal tropes—her signs—to be returned to again and again, across media, in a blended typography that was at once recognizable, common, and unique to her hand.

Unger's time at Columbia was one of joy and dogged determination. From Bladen and Sugarman, Unger gleaned the ability to manipulate metal into elongated, tensile forms that are reminiscent of the body in agitation and repose. From Niizuma, Unger gained confidence to plot out her own burgeoning system of intercultural exchanges and appropriations, finding mythic meaning in the contrasts of surface, scale, and referent. In the practice that emerges, industrial materials like builder's plaster, concrete, and metal piping are manipulated into curvilinear, anthropomorphized forms. Unger employs abstraction as an elastic, diacritical tool to underscore the semiotic and sensual enjambments between experience and ideas (fig. 1.7).

Aware of the currency of abstraction and its double bind (as a language, used to codify form; as a discourse, always exceeding its intended use), Unger began to formalize her own idioms in the mid-1970s (fig. 1.8). To the elements noted above—post-and-lintel components with both architectural and religious significance; knuckled forms evoking crossed legs, the joints of bone, and the roots of trees—she added entwined chain-link wire

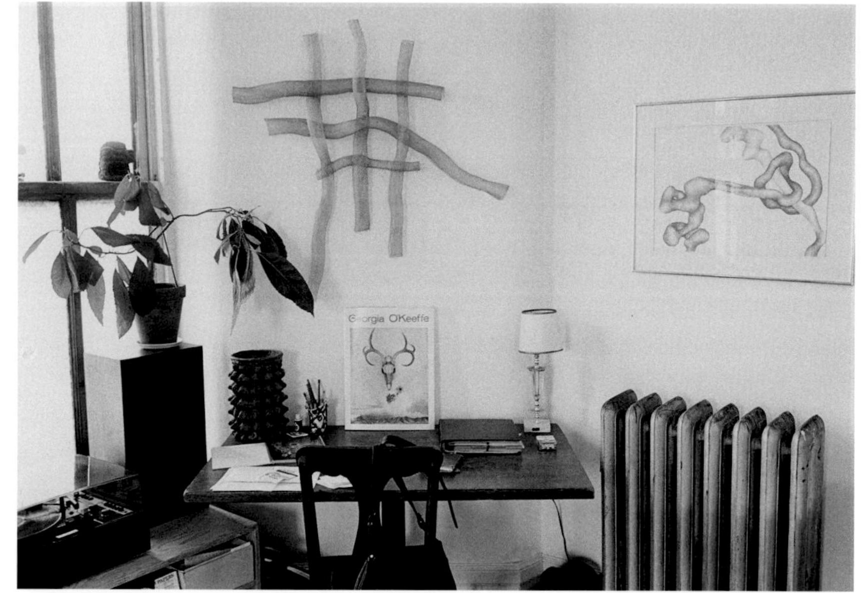

1.7
Mary Ann Unger's desk, Third Street, New York, c. 1974–75, with what looks to be a Kaish-inspired vessel, with an early *Virga* hanging above. Photo by Geoffrey Biddle. Courtesy of the artist.

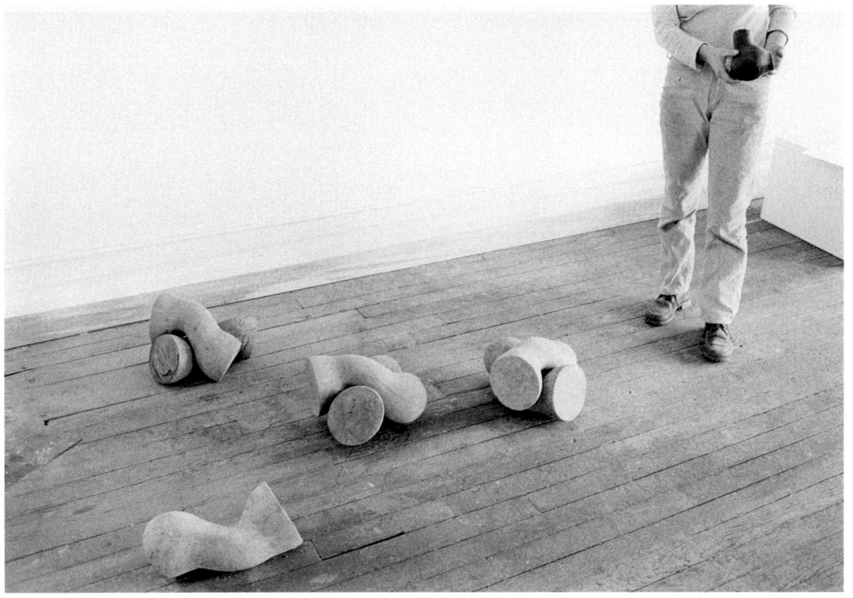

mesh. Its loops and whorls evoke construction sites, of course, but also the fluid and concrete molecular matrices of metals, water, and air that manifest both as linear equations and as matter in constant, cyclical motion between solid, liquid, and gas states. By leveraging human experience of these forms in various aspects of life, Unger is able to compound multiple references and resonances in a single "morpheme," or modular component, that she can then dial up or tone down, depending on her choice of scale, color, light, juxtaposition, and material. One can think of Unger in these formative years as a young DJ or emcee working through the component tracks of a sound kit in order to distinguish her use of abstraction from that of others. No less formal, no less geometric, but more attentive to references to the ecologies of synergy underneath our feet and our skin, Unger's expressive typographies carry a poetic-sensory awareness of material and the precision needed to inscribe the emotive and kinesthetic states of presence on positive and negative space.

Unger awakens in these years to her personal sense of sculpture as a pliant language of three dimensions. Sculpture is formal communication: a poetics in search of a common language. The modes by which sculpture not only *defines space* but also *embodies place* and, as such, brings forth

what is already inherent in the space (architectural or natural) would intrigue Unger for the remainder of her career. At Columbia, she learned how to order possibility and harness spatial sensation through her formal priorities of shifting, bending, directing, and amplifying light via rigorous examination of surface, mass, edge, and aggregated volume. Unger learned the poetic weight of a kind of sculptural haiku, as Niizuma defined it, transmuting emotional intention into formal order that allows one "to shape the moon from bone."[44] Her methodology draws out the most ineffable of emotions in the viewer while making use of a reduced palette and poignant and universal forms, through the skillful elevation of natural and industrial materials.

Arrangements
Building a Life | 1975–1985

At some point in the early 1970s, Mary Ann Unger took up the lease to a small apartment on Lafayette Street. Needing to keep within budget and buy her own supplies, while also needing to keep her skills active and her hands articulate without stiffness, Unger modified the scale of her work after graduate school and turned to working with aluminum mesh: a pliant, planar grid she could easily manipulate with bare hands and wire cutters. During this time, she began working as a research librarian in the New York photo library of Magnum Photos (then on Forty-Sixth Street between Fifth and Sixth Avenues). She maintained this job for the rest of the decade, as she hunted for a space big enough to live in and to make large-scale works. The researchers pulled Magnum members' photographs to fulfill client requests: often political journals, museum exhibitions, and news outlets.

Unger specialized in twentieth-century (then-contemporary) anthropological images; namely, ethnographic images of community life amid tribes, nations, and communities outside North America, and Indigenous coming-of-age rituals from around the world. By all accounts, Unger was adept at combing through images by the likes of Antoine d'Agata, Gregory Bateson, Werner Bischof, Rene Burri, Claude Levi-Strauss, Herbert List, Bronisław Malinowski, Margaret Mead, Inge Morath, George Rodger, and others, identifying culture and geography and explaining shamanistic practices, spiritual belief systems, and the roles and powers specific objects held in specific moments of a ritual. She seems to have been especially skilled in intuiting whether photographers had gone "internal" to do their research (become "participant-observers") or whether their images evinced a futile clinging to the still-powerful myth of objective representation. It was during such work, in the summer of 1975, that Unger met the tall, bespectacled young photographer Geoffrey Biddle, newly graduated from Harvard, who would join the ranks of the artist-researchers, with a focus on the oeuvre of Henri Cartier-Bresson. They began dating soon thereafter.

In the digital presentation of his memoir, *A Rock In A Landslide* (2020), Biddle reflects on his life with Unger, from their meeting at this moment in their lives and their practices to the twenty-three-year journey of creativity, love, illness, and parenthood that they shared before Unger's death from cancer in 1998. Especially poignant are the opening salvos of their acquaintance. Biddle recalls how, early in his time at Magnum, Unger joked with the group of researchers at the library that she had figured out the most nourishing lunch their meager salaries at the library allowed: "a can of Coca-Cola and a Hershey Bar with almonds, a rush of sugar that also managed to be sustaining." It was also Unger who made an important connection for Biddle between photographers and sculptors: both sets of makers "shared the challenge of confronting three dimensionality."[45]

A pair of untitled works from this period, dated 1975 and 1976 (figs. 1.9 and 1.10), seems to suggest Biddle and Unger's conversations regarding this challenge and acts as a harbinger of typographic attentions to come. In the earlier work, aluminum wire mesh is shaped into cylindrical fluting and then woven together to form a kind of braid that resembles the midrib of leaves or human rib bones interlaced across the sternum and

the microscopic precision of the suturing of scar tissue over a wound. In the later graphite translation of the sculpture, the textural peculiarities of tension and lassitude that provide the volume inherent within each fluted inch of mesh are now flattened into circular globules. The necessity of conforming the structure into a known shape adds mass to the drawing, while providing none of the coarse punctuation of the mesh that, conversely, adds light. But as the eye moves over both works, one cannot imagine one without the other.

The pairing speaks to the indissoluble nature of form and its translation; the two objects work alongside, not against each other. There is tension and margin, yet there is a consistent back-and-forth in the relationship between the graphic composition and the sculpture: the more closed the forms on paper, the more open and navigable they become in embodied experience.

It was not too long into Unger and Biddle's growing intimacy that she found the space she had been looking for: a sun-filled, 1,800-square-foot eighth-floor loft on Third Street off the Bowery: a former light manufacturing building across from a men's shelter and a former YMCA, which the city had repurposed for artists (the loft remains the home of the Mary Ann Unger Estate today).[46] Unger left her Lafayette Street address; Biddle left his Elizabeth Street room; and the couple moved in to the Lower East Side loft. They would wake up, go to work at Magnum, and return to the new space—sometimes meeting Unger's father, the engineer William "Bill" Unger, who would come in from New Jersey and help with running wires, installing plumbing, replacing glass, building a new bathroom, and building bookcases and cabinets. The space had a small darkroom and a spacious studio. The two artists scavenged boards, wire, and tile from building sites and abandoned buildings—making the dream of a roomy place in which to live and work comfortably in the midst of Manhattan a reality. And as Biddle and Unger settled into their new space and new routines, Unger began to experience the sculptor's tools of space and time anew: in the unities that

Ballard

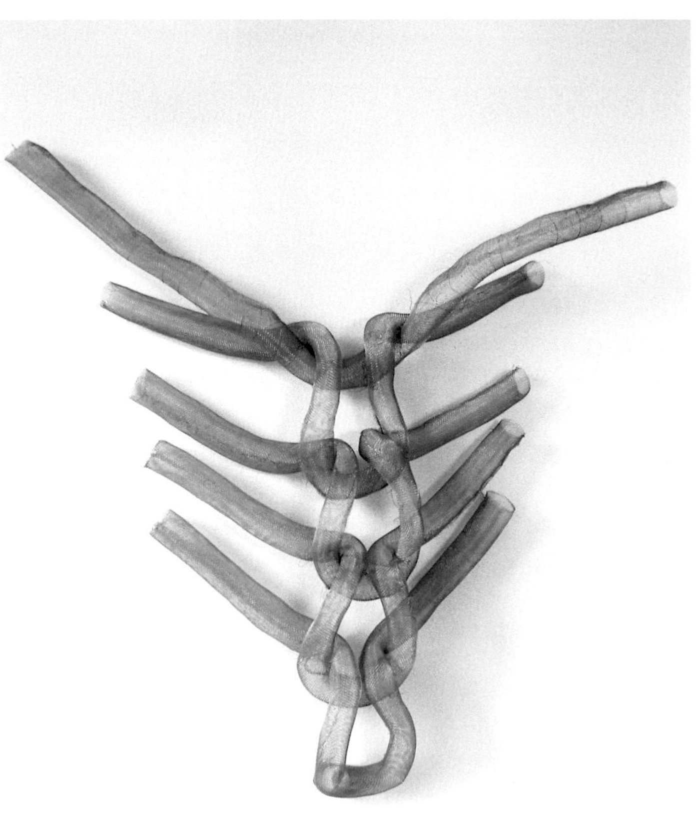

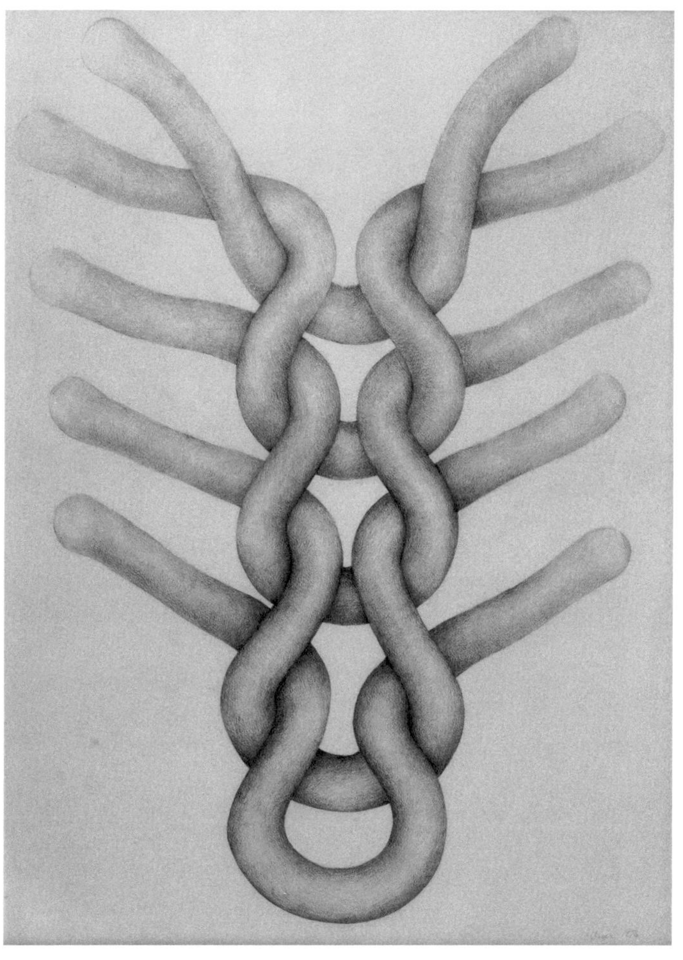

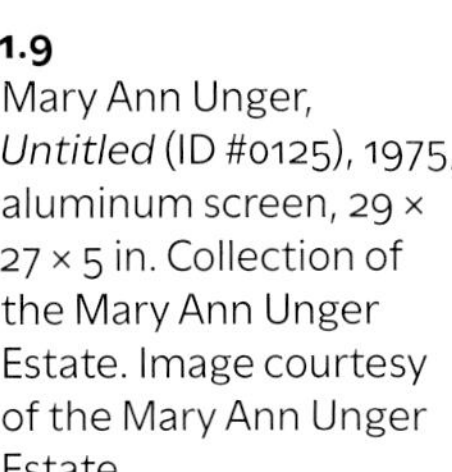

1.9
Mary Ann Unger,
Untitled (ID #0125), 1975,
aluminum screen, 29 ×
27 × 5 in. Collection of
the Mary Ann Unger
Estate. Image courtesy
of the Mary Ann Unger
Estate.

1.10
Mary Ann Unger,
Untitled (ID #0067), 1976,
graphite on paper, 30 ×
22 in. Collection of the
Mary Ann Unger Estate.
Image courtesy of the
Mary Ann Unger Estate.

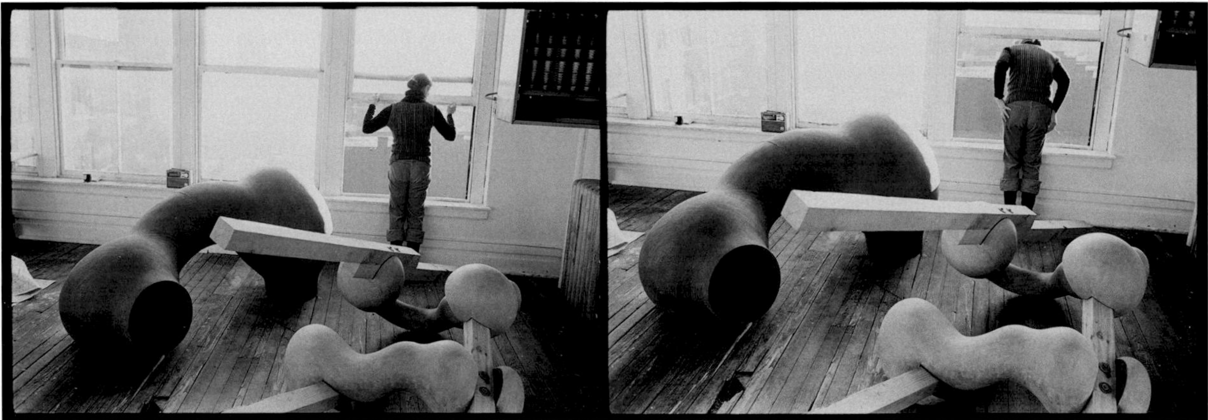

weave these two orthogonals of experience into the rounded shapes of *place*. Unger's concerns began to coalesce around now-characteristic arrangements of formal expression and scale (fig. 1.11).

The year 1977 was important for Unger as her work began to receive long-anticipated art-world attention. As noted previously, she was part of the *10 Downtown, 10 Years* exhibition at MoMA PS1 (her first and only showing at a MoMA venue to date), and she had her first two-person consideration, with painter Charlotte Hastings, at the Sycamore Gallery in Mason, Michigan. Writing about the Sycamore show for the journal *Craft Horizons* in October 1977, Louise McCagg reflected, "Unger suppresses the fluidity of clay for sculptural values, such as mass, movement, and spatial clarity. In a modular framework of molded forms, the individual units are sensually full and round… and their logical grouping or coupling in series sets up a tension between the organic and the geometric."[47] What this review, albeit brief, suggests are the material and scalar constraints Unger found herself in during the years after graduate school. Putting on hold large-scale fiberglass and plaster works supported by metal armatures, Unger was working in clay at a moderated scale and in series, thinking through sequential encounters on a table or a plinth.

Around this time, Unger became acquainted with the Colorado-based artist Clark Richert (born 1944). Their meeting was likely spurred by Richert's first New York presentation at the then-newish O.K. Harris Gallery[48] in 1978. Unger would credit Richert for introducing her to the values and uses of hexagonal and trigonal grid patterns, and he also introduced her to an extended community: the Boulder-based artists Merion Estes and Richard Kallweit, along with New York–based Gloria Klein (who became a close confidant and friend) and George Woodman. Together, these artists formed the Criss-Cross cooperative: a group of painters and printmakers inspired by Buckminster Fuller's assertion that the human body "was defined not by its materiality, but by the patterning of its materials."[49] In this vein, the Criss-Cross artists studied and replicated the forms of DNA and other structural patterns, such as fractals, to get at broader structural patterns that were "objective" (we might use the words *endemic* or *inherent* now) but not necessarily visual—like inequality based on gender and race—and the evocative power of musical notation. Kallweit's dictum that these patterned works "were not *about* something, they *were* something" galvanized these artists to use grid-based patterns as means to form a system of transitive augmentations and transferable "modules" or intervals. The artist wishing to reference global and historical modes of decoration, myth, and cultural fluency could then replicate these elements as a postmodern tool in order to index, re-create, and then apply "universal structures" of alignment and affinity.[50]

Working with the Criss-Cross artists in ways that were material and theoretical, patterned but highly linguistic and abstract, may well have reminded Unger of her college days in

1.11
Mary Ann Unger looking out the window, Third Street, New York, c. 1974–75. Photo by Geoffrey Biddle. Courtesy of the artist.

Ballard

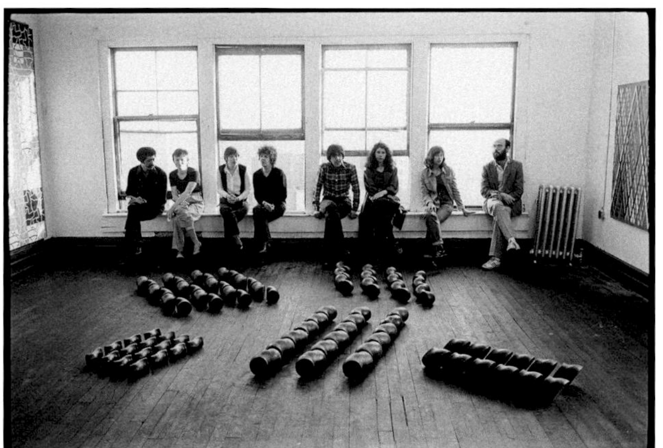

The Well (1979), a bonded-iron, twenty-piece circular work sited on Ward's Island on the East River in New York, seems a transformative sculpture that functions, in hindsight, as a bridge between Unger's graduate study and the commissions that followed (fig. 1.13). The chicken-wire and metal-rod armatures are now welded steel, and the materials are now industrial grade and meant for all-weather use. Unger had publicly expressed a deep interest in systems and patterning and the use of mathematical notation to aid her translations between paper grids, material maquettes, a broader "floor plan" of an object, and the to-scale armature forms. Systems and patterning, she believed, gave a kind of structure that was rhythmic. But something new began to happen in the 1980s, and *The Well* indicates the tonal shift of Unger's thinking. In an artist's talk she gave for the New York–based series Artists Talk on Art, in the winter of 1980, Unger referenced *The Well* by saying, "Orderly structure is important…. There's also something else that's happening and it's emotional, this idea of a circular form that's somewhat non-patterned…. Whereas its individual units may have a pattern, the whole to me is important, and it's a little bit different than the parts, the system of parts."[51] Unger readily acknowledged that even this new way of thinking about more rounded, curvilinear lines and forms that provide immediacy and emotive energy was based on mathematical precision. "I placed the forms on the floor somewhat intuitively and then realized [the pieces] did actually correspond to a grid, and then I made the drawing, the plan…. This is a cast form and again, it involves some mathematics, if you're going to have 20 units, you have to divide a circle into twenty pie-shapes that are the same." However, Unger goes on, the circular form, as glyph that formally conveys emotion and meaning, must work to maintain "proportionately and somewhat intuitively in its attempt to describe"; it is useless unless it is

Hadley and the importance of the graphic gesture for sculptors and painters alike. Richert, and later Woodman, would ask Unger to contribute articles and interviews for the Criss-Cross publications. In 1979–80, with Richert and several other Criss-Cross artists, Unger curated a show and lecture series at her loft on East Third Street during the winter season when both the Hansen Gallery and the O.K. Harris Works Gallery had presentations of Richert's work on view, and the artist had come to New York for an extended stay (fig. 1.12).

Through Richert's introduction of multidimensional, nonhierarchical pattern-making techniques that sought to extend abstract, but integrated, principles of cosmology and connection beyond the picture plane, Unger's biomorphic abstraction (still closely tied to the human figure) received another layer of possible remove. These experimental superimpositions—the permutations, aleatory inversions, and mathematically based algorithms to determine forms and their colors—stretched her practice and motivated her to build a practice of standardized sequences rather than consistent attentions or narratives. Unger began in this moment to work out early strands of ideas on hexagonal and trigonal patternings of her own making—layered grids in graphite, ink, and pigment—to inform the way her eyes and hands came to wire mesh. While the Criss-Cross artists were largely painters working in two dimensions, Unger saw and realized the possibility of using these patterned experiments to move with intention from drawings to three-dimensional forms at heroic scale.

useful in the building of a module within a specific language that can index both "presence and what it means to be away."[52]

Coming just a few years after she settled in the Third Street loft, Unger's remarks suggest that the resolution of a multiyear search for "home" animated her ability to articulate her intentions and begin to redirect and sharpen her thinking. Unger began to consider her process both serially and sequentially and refined what it looked like for her, as a maturing artist, to carry certain things forward and set other attentions aside, trusting—as she had a few years earlier when funds were tight and materials limited—that if the source material were resonant enough, she could return to those patterns. It is not surprising, then, that just months after this new articulation of purpose and planning (and settledness) Unger was awarded the first of her fellowships at Yaddo in Saratoga Springs.

In his memoir and in correspondence, Biddle relays how the period of the late 1970s and early 1980s raised the important and expected conversations and negotiations between partners—when/if to move in together, when/if to marry, when/if to start a family—to the level of politics. These life-altering decisions were negotiated daily, over months, over years, in the midst of expanding practices, between Biddle's out-of-town photojournalism assignments and Unger's commissions for site-specific installations across the region, and within the particular sociopolitical conversation around gender equality in the art world. Unger was committed to feminist discourses and collective action. She believed deeply in making space for other female artists (often quickly turning the loft into a gallery space, and a party into a viewing) and found ways of asserting her own expertise in the decidedly male-dominated niche of post-Minimalist sculpture. She also regularly mentored other young female artists in how to negotiate for themselves with critics and galleries.[53]

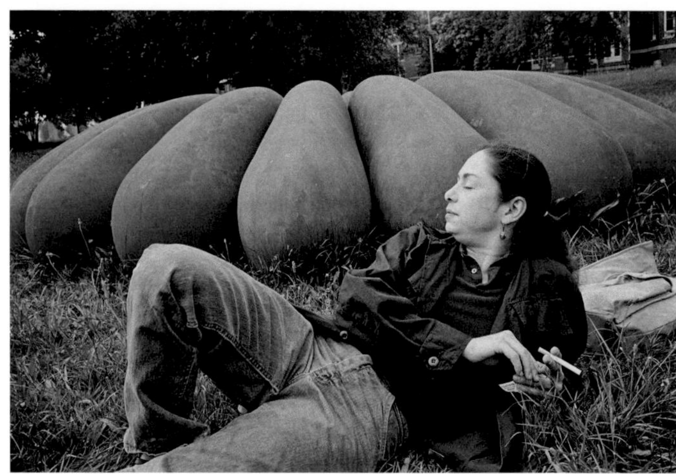

Though domestic and professional fulfillment are often cast by the scarcity rhetoric promulgated by societal structures of white supremacy and misogyny as either/or propositions, and, sometimes, experienced as such in moments of decision, Unger found a way to build a home, to build a family, and to build a practice in the midst of internal and external pressures—space and time to work being chief among them. Unger wanted to start a family, yet she was deeply moved by the assertion of several feminist luminaries that the demands of a nuclear family were misaligned with the work of equity. And while Unger and Biddle did marry in 1980, and welcomed their daughter in 1982 (fig. 1.14), she continued to amplify the voices of women and femme-expressing artists, especially those living and taking part in the Lower East Side art scene.

Unger mentored other women holding similar longings and facing similar pressures. She continued to create community by hosting regular gatherings of artists,

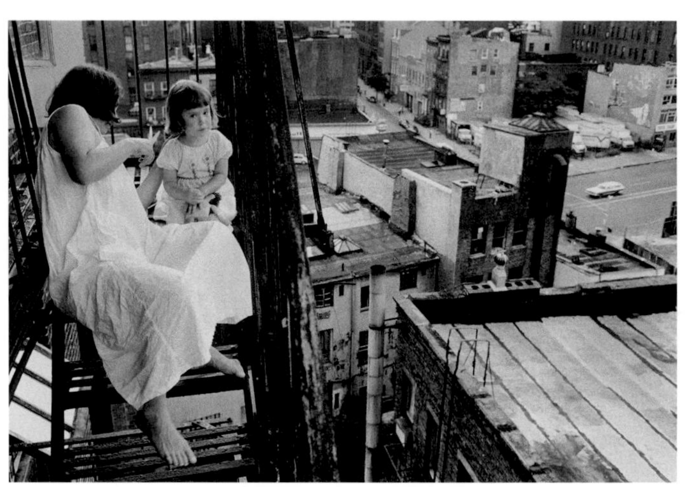

students, critics, and curators from various parts of her life and at all stages of their careers. In these moments, she regularly gave over large sections of the loft for viewings, leaning into the practice of continuing her own material experimentations while making space for others and sharing her skills in welding and cutting. Biddle and Unger often hosted artist friends and collaborators in the loft to share meals and refine skills. Discussion inevitably turned to the "artist's dream" of representation in a commercial gallery, a museum presentation, and a decent review: the trifecta of artistic attainment that begins to signal the transition from working a day job while making work to having the ability to focus on one's study, experimentation, and making full-time.

Legacy | 1985–1998

Sometime between 1985 and 1987, Unger joined the Guerrilla Girls in their collective fight to call out and subvert sexism and racism in all facets of the art world. In a recent recounting of that now-legendary shared epiphany among seven female artists gathered, in the spring of 1985, to protest the Museum of Modern Art's *International Survey of Recent Painting and Sculpture*, inaugurating the museum's renovated and expanded building (which was neither international nor inclusive), member "Käthe Kollwitz" recalls:

> People thought that museums were meritocracies—that if you were good enough, you were in, and if you weren't, you were out. But we knew from our own world of artists . . . we knew that that simply was not true. And there was also, at that moment, our "a-ha" moment, which is why the Guerrilla Girls still exist today: the idea that there had to be an in-your-face, disruptive, better way to convince people that the art world was a patriarchy, and the work of white males was valued, and the work of women and artists of color was thought to be not up to the standards of the art world. . . . So we

> had the idea to do posters about this; to try to show people what was really going on.[54]

It is easy to see how such considered and collective fearlessness, such righteous anger and frustration directed so consequentially against hegemonic masculinity, unified by an iconic gorilla/guerilla "mask-ulinity," appealed to Unger. The dark humor and the fun of it all. The getting into "good trouble." As "Frida Kahlo" asserts, "The masks are key as it doesn't matter who we are, really. It's really very useful in the art world to have an alter-ego… to realize the dynamic of power and connection in the art world."[55] As an early member of the group, Unger helped to shape the transition from museum critique and statistics shared on posted flyers and multiples to the group's own program of exhibitions and the critique of scholars.

In the last years of Unger's practice, her intentions as an artist and her attentions as a curator began to offer new interventions in space and expanded networks across the trans-Hudson region. Alongside the exciting shifts toward monumentality in her constructions in the mid-1980s, she began to extend her curatorial practice. As Geoffrey Biddle writes, Unger clung to the dream of "a brave future" of making a living from her work (fig. 1.15), but saw her broader practice as having emotive and critical import beyond her own hand.[56] During the late 1970s, Unger had been offering space and curating dialogues between people and objects. The 1980s saw her asked to plan and guest-curate several presentations at the Sculpture Center and the Trans Hudson Gallery's Manhattan location.[57]

While agitating to make space for all kinds of good work by women artists and artists of color that was not being seen and regularly reviewed, Unger was diagnosed with breast cancer in 1985. The aggregate of a more-formalized curatorial turn, with the Guerrilla Girls, with a chronic diagnosis, marks 1985 as a defining year in Unger's life and practice. These separate but interlinked impetuses for personal and communal reflection catalyzed Unger's drive toward a cache of refined and

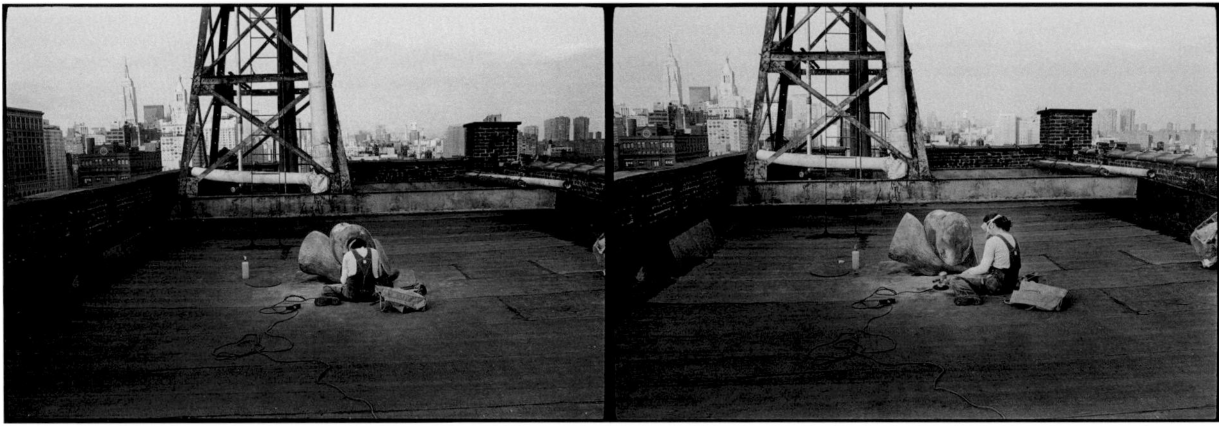

formidable works across multiple disciplines, which are explored in the following section. While 1985 began with the world-changing event of the diagnosis and the realities of surgery and chemotherapy, the year ended, that November, with Unger's first reviewed curated group exhibition, *The Figure as an Image of the Psyche*, at the Sculpture Center (which was then at 167 East Sixty-Ninth Street).

The twelve-artist show included work by Sydney Blum, Roland Briseno, Jonathan Ellis, Greer Lankton, Mary Malott, Natan Nuchi, Scott Richter, Italo Scanga, Theodora Skipitares, Nancy Spero, Augusta Talbot, and Unger. The show's organizing principle was the ways contemporary sculptors were interrogating the human figure as a site "to confront and transform difficult and some-times extreme responses and experiences," from the personal event to collective reckon-ing.[58] Acknowledging that the show's thesis and the works were "present[ing] a very different view of Expressionism than the one prevalent now," Michael Brenson (in his review for the *New York Times*) wrote that Unger's selections serve as "reminders that declaratory emotional statements are always possible."[59] Though she had been mentioned in the *Times* in connection with previous shows, Brenson's review gave Unger her first public mention as a curator, as well as the first full-throated endorsement of her practice via Brenson's affective engagement with the large-form 1985 work *Supplicant* (fig. 1.16).

The Sculpture Center invited Unger back in 1986 for a full staging of her four-part installation of structures and attendant forms titled *Communion*. Unger accomplished this important solo project in between two mastectomies and the beginning of chemo-therapy. Writing for the *Times*, Brenson observed that Unger "is clearly drawn both to something ideal and contemplative, perhaps identified here with the Orient, and to the pain and violence of the world."[60] (A subse-quent essay in this volume reflects on Unger's use of non-Western forms.) What is striking in this 1986 moment is that Brenson begins to articulate what Unger's influences and attentions have led to: "the two sides of her sculpture…. The cool, architectural side… and the expressive."[61]

The last years of the 1980s brought ever-growing regional acclaim and the opportu-nity to jury a group of works for the Newhouse Center for Contemporary Art at Snug Harbor on Staten Island, the A.I.R. Gallery "Invitational" of 1988, and a return to the Sculpture Center for a curated conversa-tion of artists and their works titled *In a Dark Vein*. The end of the decade also delivered heartbreak. By 1989, Unger's cancer had returned as cancer of the bone. The artist and her family were preparing for the cancer's eventual progression into the brain and the loss of motor function. The end of the decade inaugurated a second chapter of chemo-therapy and hormone suppressants, which altered Unger's physical appearance and made predicting and planning for the periods of great productivity and periods of much-needed rest all the more difficult, even impossible. Regular and extended sojourns

1.15
Mary Ann Unger using a disc sander on the roof, Third Street, New York, c. 1977. Photo by Geoffrey Biddle. Courtesy of the artist.

Ballard

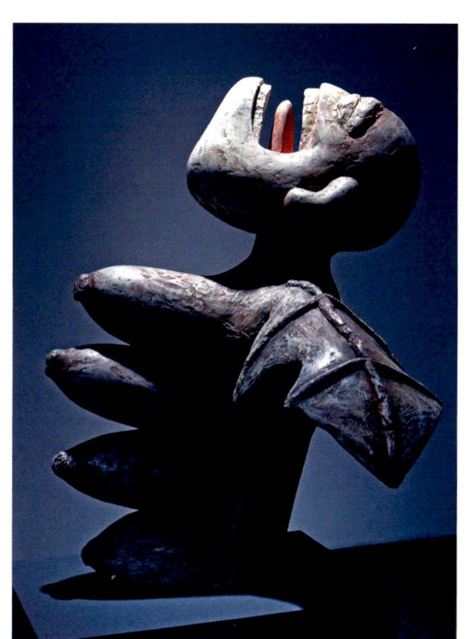

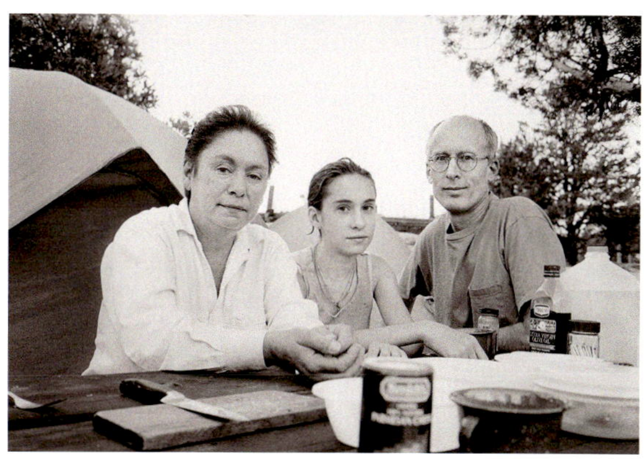

outside the city to a house upstate in Wallkill, New York, plus traveling and visiting with family and friends between the Jersey suburbs and Maine, made the 1990s as elastic, restorative, and conducive to making work as time would allow.

Critics noted that by 1985, a "darker vein" had already permeated Unger's forms. But in 1989 and 1990, with the time and space given by her first Pollock-Krasner Foundation fellowship, then her Athena Fellowship and a grant from the New York Foundation of Arts, respectively, we begin to see her heretofore modular, geometric, and grid-based forms elongate into truly "dark, bulbous, beamlike forms… with surfaces that appeared to be scarred and scorched, suggest[ing] the aftermath of some mysterious ritual or catastrophe."[62] These works, in their full flower, were on view in Unger's winter-to-spring solo presentation at the Klarfeld Perry Gallery in 1992.

The works in this show, titled *Dark Icons*, synthesize the mid-eighties threads of architectural surround and expressive, conceptual form. In these works, Greco-Roman myth and Judeo-Christian parable inform the abstract structuring of oblong, rhizomatic arrangements of arma-tured forms overlaid with pigmented Hydrocal. It is in this moment, through the working out and arrang-ing of works such as *Pall Bearers* (1989) and *Deposition / Nature Mourned* (1991, see fig. 3.5), that Unger comes upon the overarching theme of migration—across cultures, across geographies, across the bounds of life and death—that informs her colossal master-piece, the installation *Across the Bering Strait* (1992–94, see figs. 3.1–3.4), which debuted in 1994 in the Trans Hudson Gallery space in Jersey City, New Jersey.

In the summer of 1996, Unger, Biddle, and fourteen-year-old Eve took one last major trip together to the Four Corners region where Arizona, Colorado, New Mexico, and Utah come together (fig. 1.17). This would be Unger's final travel outside the Hudson Valley region. (Eighteen months later, the disease had altered her physical capacities and greatly reduced her language function.) Though the family had intended to drive and camp throughout the trip, it was clear Unger tired easily. They stayed in a small, two-room stucco house in Taos owned by Biddle's uncle and aunt, Sydney and Flora Biddle. Artists routinely stopped by and joined the quintet for meals. On one such occasion, Sydney and Flora's eighty-four-year-old neighbor, the painter Agnes Martin, stopped by and sat beside Mary Ann.

At the table, sharing food and space under the sun, in the glare of white light in dry air, Martin reveled in Unger's attention. Unger delighted in Martin's earthiness. Both so conversant yet measured in their respective spatial dictums and material experimenta-tion. Both practices arising from the possibili-ties and the constraints of the personal. Both so adept at ways to make abstraction based on the grid, expansive and poetic. In this moment, they spoke of New York and what it meant to be away from "her." Martin shared how, on having a dream thirty years earlier, where she made a simple adobe brick by hand and then built a structure with that brick and others that appeared before her, she moved west. Unger was riveted.[63]

What Remains | Oeuvre

Mary Ann Unger's practice arises from the possibilities and constraints of the personal. Unger negotiates the ways by which cultural myth, disease, and the sociostructural impositions on women and women's bodies traverse society and self. Unger's life and art provide an example of a postmodern self-seeking and delighting in the cross-pollination of "shifting ideas and materials across forms and medium," rather than hiding or "cynically skewering politics, history, identity, biography" in order to "make a case for its own existence."[64]

An expressive formalist attuned to the nuanced application of patterning, surface texture, internal mass, and the use of color to delineate the edge of where a passage or zone of a plane meets the surrounding air, Unger consistently embraced the tensions between graphic regularity and the rigors of play and mutability. Across her maturing practice, she was able to translate experiences of pain and repair into an expressive typography of elements that could be interchanged and intermixed to create powerful installations that said something poignant about existence and reckoning with pain.

By 1980, Unger was beginning to define her practice as turning a corner from the work of the 1970s. Her lyrical and intuitive sense of communicative principles during this period offers a kind of pleasure-play and formal abundance through the ways in which her varying compositions regularly demonstrate a preoccupation with shape over line, surface texture over color, and an intuitive sense of dimension and scale that invites human encounter.

I now turn to distinguishing the arrangements, or modes,[65] of Unger's expressive and protoconceptual practice.[66] Her work from the late 1970s until her death in 1998 can be parsed in as many ways as there are viewers. That multiplicity and identification with the self is the point of her expression. Yet for the purposes of this broad reconsideration of her life and practice, it feels right to offer as comprehensive a container as possible for the works. As such, I propose that we think of Unger's compositions within seven loose and symbiotic arrangements (the "floor plans" or preparatory drawings for many of the commissions notwithstanding) corresponding to installation technique, as much as to materials, time, theme, and scale. These "arrange-

ments" can be listed within three material modes as follows:

WORKS ON PAPER
Attentions (1978–98)
Elementals (1983–88)

VOTIVE BRONZES
Fragments (1986–93)

ARMATURE STRUCTURES
Virgas (c. 1974–80)
Site-Specific Commissions (1978–96)
Engagements, i.e., the series *Mitosis / Wishing Stones* and *Vertebrae* (1982–98)
Monuments (1985–94)

Unger worked across media and materials, returning and eliding distinctions as it pleased her attentions and, later, as it felt most possible to follow an idea through pain and fatigue. As she matured, and as the disease made consistent reliance on her own capacity less certain, she worked with a number of assistants, the artists Daniel Carello, Greer Lankton, and Jim Gowans among them. After the first Yaddo residency, Unger boasted a steady stream of fellowships and residencies that indicate maturation and critical interest, despite gaps for rest, treatment, and family time.

The Davidson Gallery[67] in New York has mounted three presentations of Unger's work to date, including two beautiful presentations of her Attentions. These works on paper constitute a series of Richert-esque open-and-shut positions, impositions, and tessellations useful throughout Unger's mature practice. Neither preliminary sketches nor formal etudes, they come sometimes before but mostly after a corresponding effort of "working out" the theme in material (fig. 1.18). In the late 1970s and increasingly as the 1980s progressed, these works begin to shift, the element of color and volume superseding line, graphite or colored pencil being augmented with watercolor and even Crayola markers. Once exacting and almost architectural in their graphic relation to volume, the works

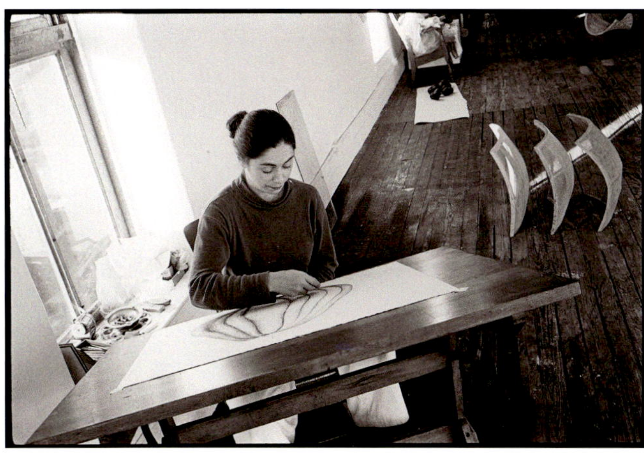

1.18
Mary Ann Unger drawing, Third Street, New York, 1977. Photo by Geoffrey Biddle. Courtesy of the artist.

1.19
Mary Ann Unger, *Untitled (Study for Hexagonal Quintet)* (ID #1151), 1978, watercolor and pencil on paper, 20½ × 26¾ in. Collection of the Mary Ann Under Estate. Image courtesy of the Mary Ann Unger Estate.

1.20
Mary Ann Unger [with Virgas], c. 1979–81. Photo by Geoffrey Biddle. Courtesy of the artist.

become flatter as color is added, much more idiomatic of the series of engagements with color and linear economy that Josef Albers had taught in his foundational class at Black Mountain College (fig. 1.19).[68]

Over and over again, Unger plays with figure-ground relationships, negative and positive spaces, and color contrasts to energize her cascading typographical compositions in graphite, ink, and color pencil. She regularly imposes a self-made grid (often triangular) atop commercial graph paper or a hand-drawn square grid, permitting the mismatch and elisions to spur her toward sensuous foldings and biomorphic, if knuckled or hairlike, enjambments. This imposition of the triangular axis upon the square plane allows Unger to leverage the grid in order to push past (or, in contemporary parlance, "to queer") abstraction in a curious but important give and take. The resulting works offer a resolved interplay between spatial and conceptual tensions, a fluidity between the figure patterning and the ground where both alternately emerge and recede, and a unique typography of hierarchies, resolutions, inverted shapes and signs, and unconscious compositions.

The early works of aluminum mesh I term the Virgas (from the Latin for rod, stripe, wand) are lyric economies of crenellated form (fig. 1.20). Unger bent, shaped, wove, pulled, and folded sheets or strips of the metal grid matrix into a volumetric parameter, often resembling handmade ceramic vessels, fragments of stone ornament, or natural dimensional forms like carapaces and honeycomb. A kind of rigorous play, the Virgas allowed Unger to keep exploring the relationship of causation between surface and shape, and between an object's skein and its mass. The Virgas also clarify the progression of an idea from handheld wire mesh to the architectural forms of the maquettes for the sited public commissions. These ten- to twenty-inch manipulations with wire cutter and bare hands share affinity with the graphic Attentions; indeed, as in the case of the untitled pair of 1975/76 (see figs. 1.9–1.10), the Virga form catalyzed the later drawing.

Beginning in the years immediately following her pregnancy, and continuing through the mid-1980s as she struggled with the realities of a breast cancer diagnosis, there are a loose series of drawings and prints on paper featuring a columnar subject, with exaggerated breasts, bones, and cupped hands, with a jagged howling mouth, yawping, pleading to an omniscient power beyond the edge of the composition (see fig. 1.16). I term these works en masse, centered around a print series titled *Amazon*, and numbered with roman numerals, the Elementals. The Elementals are a kind of ponderous biomorphic glyph with teeth and sometimes hands, lifted in the orant pose of supplication, grief, or cupping breasts.

The Elementals clarify how Unger the artist is synthesizing the compounded roles of Unger-as-mother and Unger-as-lover and

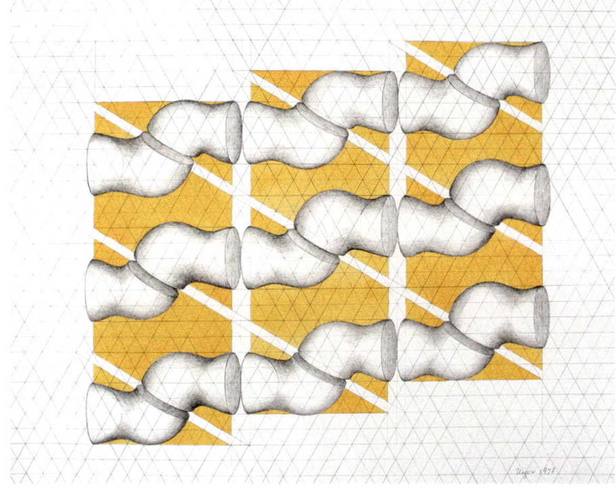

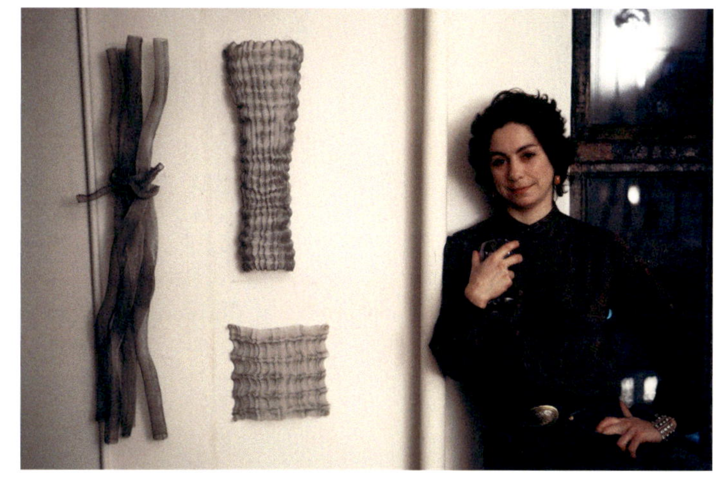

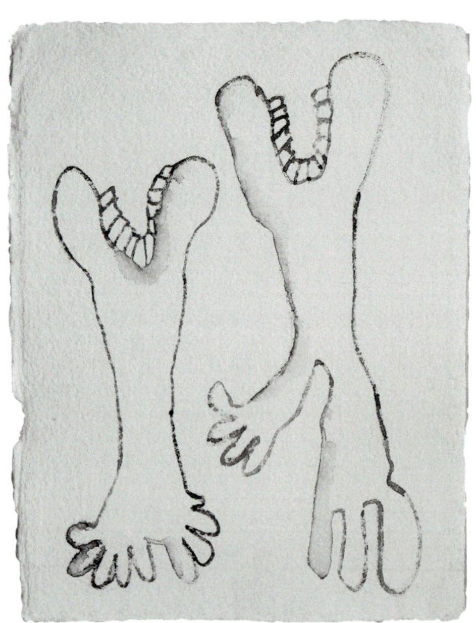

Unger-as-patient. All told, these works traverse the predicament of a unified sense of self in the presence of pain. In a 1994 artist talk, Unger spoke about Picasso's *Guernica* (1937) as a kind of ever-present eidolon in her mind during the period of genesis of the Elementals. Since her early days as a child attending art classes at the Museum of Modern Art, that painting had been in permanent residence on the third floor. Now, in this extended moment of flux for Unger, the painting, which had been a constant artistic companion and a beacon of how an artist creates out of grief and anti-war fervor, was returning to Spain.[69] The resonance between the upturned, U-shaped maws in Unger's work, which recall question marks with teeth, and the faces of anger, rage, and grief at the cardinal points of *Guernica* is palpable. Once imagined, the accord is hard not to see (fig. 1.21).

The Elementals emerged in a period of Unger's life when there were big questions and no forthcoming answers. And we can see the artist working it through: Where or in which formal element does memory and emotive evocation reside? Is it color? Is it the line? Is it patterning and texture? Is it in asymmetry? Is it in citation? Is it in proportion? Is it in contoured shade? Is it in a combination of these things and, if so, which combinations? And while I maintain that neither the

Attentions nor the Elementals are studies in the traditional sense, they are instructive for understanding how Unger moves from elaborate ideation to material form, and back again, crisscrossing media and scalar attentions, while keeping certain syntactical identifiers of sculpture—edge, space, proportion, shadow—at the fore. The Elementals contrast the joint delineating elements of line, color, and mass (a thick black line) with the discursive and cyclical nature of memory, and visualize a mode, albeit fleeting, wherein Unger tries to hold the seen and the unknown in balance.

Spanning the period between 1986 and 1994 (which included her first Pollock-Krasner Fellowship in 1989 and a Guggenheim Fellowship in 1992), Unger created a rueful and poignant series of approximately fifty sculptural confrontations à la Giacometti's standing corpses and Max Ernst's chess players *avec le diable*. In sum, the *Fragments* are a series of bronze, votive-size torsos depicting a range of human emotions through essential gestures of motherhood or canonical positions of the tortured or diseased body in art (fig. 1.22; see fig. 2.6). These bronze works were created from a lost-wax process, with initial models constructed of hard, brown wax supported by found sticks and bits of driftwood Unger foraged while on vacation during family trips to the Maine coast. Close reflection reveals the profound influence of George Sugarman's linear contraction of the body with an eye toward Louise Bourgeois's semiotic organs. Unlike Giacometti's, these are not full forms, nor do they rival human scale. Just larger than the space of Unger's hand, the warm metal skeins present pockmarked surfaces that bear the impression of being knuckled, punched, pressed, bitten, kneaded, and palmed.

Rosalind Krauss's criticism, especially the late-1980s examinations of Bourgeois's "partial-forms,"[70] feels contextually relevant. Krauss was in search of a kind of *écriture féminine* that centered not on the phallus as

1.21
Mary Ann Unger, *Untitled* (ID #1430), c. 1996, watercolor on paper, 12½ × 9½ in. Courtesy of the Mary Ann Unger Estate. Image courtesy of the Mary Ann Unger Estate.

1.22
Mary Ann Unger, *Fragments Series, No. 51*, 1993, bronze, 17 × 9½ × 3 in. Collection of the Mary Ann Unger Estate. Image courtesy of the Mary Ann Unger Estate.

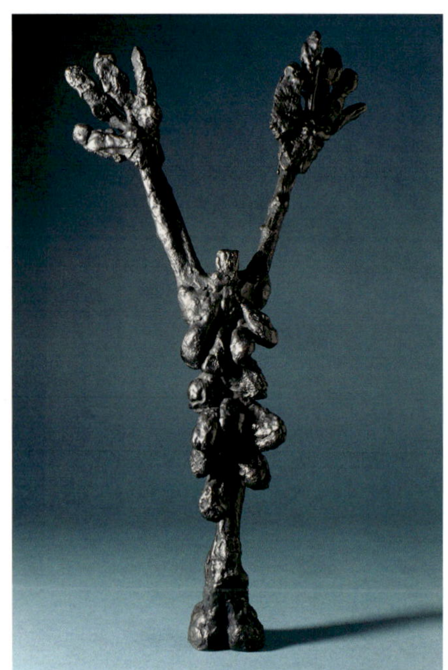

Ballard

representational signifier but on the truncation of the torso or bust to its most essential and timeless synecdoches. Rather than phallus or menhir as human primordial or ur-text, Krauss, via Bourgeois, offered the body as gut, the body as shapely and shapeless breasts, the body as hands, the body as thighs. These pairs of muscles that move us and also sustain life, Krauss deems, collapse the individual shape of the phallus into a footnote to the historical acts (which speak volumes, but are yet to be written about in volumes) of the limbs that bear weight and stretch and strain in childbirth and in the act of love. Unger's *Fragments* are thus a highly formal matter, tapped into what Alice Neel calls "the deep vein of feeling of one's moment."[71] The most traditionally figurative of Unger's extant works, they function—through their theorization and expression of anguish and aesthetic citation—as some of the most "abstract" works that survive her.

The *Fragments* are also important as they impinge upon a topic taken up in a subsequent essay in this volume, on the sense of Unger's aesthetic appropriation from prehistoric and non-Euro-American cultures. And while the geometric extrapolations of Brancusi's votives from West Africa are not legible in these works per se, there is the similar sense that Unger is using figurative votive forms to massage the wordplay between a woman's bust and the bust portrait as a commodity and signal of individual cultural status, and as the site of multiple dis-eases, from cancer to the male gaze. The remix happening here is theoretically dense and rich. In this light, the *Fragments* are a declaration against gesture, though their gestural specificities elicit a playful rigor that is both caricature and political invective in a kind of weird hat tip to Honoré Daumier, Edvard Munch, and Rodin, against the critical and literary blazoning of the female body. For all they hold, the *Fragments* are understandably deeply turbulent objects of power, pocketed and imprinted with the pressures of fingertips, palette knives, and knuckles. While the language of the sublime is not quite useful—at its core it entails a momentary fear of self-subsumption or annihilation in the

presence, or on the precipice, of immeasurable plentitude or void—there is an overwhelming intensity of transfer here. One can sense an artist whose hand is curling, poking, prodding, beating, banging, palming, kneading soft-warm bronze, working the muscles as to relax. The *Fragments* function as art and as stress test for a body changing, not always capable of working each day at the scale, and for the stakes, desired. Their minuscule but finely articulated limbs sunder the air around them, giving them a presence and power that belies their stature. There is something arresting and humbling, personal and unnerving about the silence of an object so obviously sensate and sonic, *Der Schrei der Natur* indeed.[72]

There is resonance in the figurative schema between the Elementals on paper and the *Fragments* in material; however, like so much of Unger's extant work and her thinking, rhythms and analogies seem more apt than comparisons, correlations, or matches, especially given the dates and range of media. More apt to say Unger's mind and hand returned often to resonant archetypes that yielded similar visual tropes across media and scale. And in the *Fragments*, even as Unger is pushing past the redacted language of Minimalism, she still provides an economy of form and a clear attention to materials and their latitude of inside/outside, positive surface/negative space. Meant to sit on tabletops or shelves, the *Fragments* intersect with the margins of what is furniture and what is architecture by intervening and interacting with space and surfaces, delineating new, melting shapes against whatever architectural enclosures within or outside of which they may exist. It is as if, like minkisi or katsina dolls, the bronze figures offer channels of communication above and below ground, from beyond the boundary of life itself.

The third and most critically received mode of Unger's practice to date has been the armature-supported structures from just before 1980 until the end of her career. As Unger introduced herself and her recent intentions during an artist talk in the winter of 1980: "I'm a sculptor and my most recent work is probably the closest to patterning and crisscrossing concerns…. The work is about structure and it comes out of my work with armatures. My work used to be much fuller, there were under-structures…. These were discarded in casting more solid, massive forms."[73] Varying in complexity and scale across her practice, these works are either engaged, meaning they lock or notch into a substrate (floor or wall), or are free-standing sculpture resting on the floor or ground sans plinth.

During her pregnancy in 1981, Unger began hiring assistants and working out a "new system" of fabrication. And while this new mode of working distanced her hand from some of the specific encounters with material she craved, it bolstered her ability to speak cogently to other artists and to critics and curators about the work and its concerns in medias res. The refined, systemic process of Unger's mature oeuvre consisted of first producing an im/positional drawing (perhaps an Attention), then intuitively working out the armature form in eight-inch welding rod or manipulated mesh; then, she would create a new "floor plan" or study for a work that was primarily concerned with the formal qualities of negative/positive space and edge, and finally coat the armature with plaster, clay, or, increasingly, Hydrocal, according to the floor plan. "These underneath structures [of a work] have always been very interesting to me," she noted, and in the years of commu-nity with the Criss-Cross artists (1978–85), Unger came to realize that "I had been using sloppy armatures!" She discovered that the sentience, power, and mass she wanted were not a result of "slathering more and more plaster on them" or having an "overbuilt" armature but, in fact, a want of more sophisti-cated armatures "based on the grid drawings with their patternings and weavings."[74] Throughout the remaining years of her practice, the grid, which could hold and support both the scalar and the narrative contours of an idea, remained "a primary concern of mine."[75]

The bulk of Unger's public art projects were commissioned during the mid to late 1980s, and were extant in situ by 1991.[76] The grid is so central to these works that they are all, regardless of material or scale, exposed armatures, open to the elements and the encounter/interaction with passersby, insects, and sound. The multilateral part-beehive, part-Palladian-rococo rotunda that is *Temple* (1986) at Ursinus College in College-town, Pennsylvania, is perhaps most indica-tive of Unger's new system of working in the mid-1980s. The roof is a series of punctuated painted aluminum parabolas that cascade like waterworks, formed of interlocking 45-degree equatorial triangles conceived on the imposition of several grids. The model was completed in 1985 and the work fabri-cated and installed in 1986. *Beehive Temple* (1987), installed in the botanical gardens of Lehigh University in Bethlehem, Pennsylvania, is on a similar plane, but more vertical and informed less by architectural ideals and more by the hexagonal tessellations in the natural world, especially larkspur, beehives, and ears of corn.

Contemplating Unger's site-specific installation *Tweed Garden* (1985) at Tweed Courthouse in New York, Michael Brenson, again writing for the *New York Times*, called the ten painted, nine-foot hexagonal columns resembling both trees and the clerestory pillars of a cathedral's side aisle "heavy with meaning," as well as "ornamental and light." He wrote, "This work is very easy to be with, yet it is substantial enough to be around for a while."[77] Brenson seems to suggest that site-specific, environmental installations are either a delight or "substantial," which I take to mean important, which I take to mean self-aware and referential to their formal lineage. But Unger's neoexpressionist efforts surprised, if not delighted, Brenson by being both. *This* does not surprise. Unger is a consummate orchestrator of space and form, specifically as she considers light and egress just as important to large-scale installation as shape and volume.

But perhaps more than any of her other nine public commissions, the last, *Ode to Tatlin* (1991) for the Aaron Copland School of Music at Queens College in Flushing, New York, proves the most resolved and unified (fig. 1.23). From above looking down onto the work, the eye would see a steel ellipse halved with a main ambulatory through the center, but at a direct angle onto the work, the radial egress ways between the steel beams allow the light to refract and glitter off the polished surfaces as students, faculty, staff, musicians, patrons, and the curious pass in and out. It is a plan that references both the crown of the Statue of Liberty and Michelangelo's original curved design for the Campidoglio. From the street walking up the steps, one could discern the nineteen-foot installation's referent to the alto and bass clefs, and the steel staves as bars of musical notation.[78] Walking through the sculpture from the Copland School out onto Kissena Boulevard in Flushing, one would see an edifice reaching out to the steel-and-glass city beyond its doors, encircling, drawing that sound, that flavor, inside. In *Ode to Tatlin*, Unger achieves (perhaps, more aptly than any of the other Criss-Cross affiliated artists) universal structures of alignment and affinity at a macro scale.

Though Unger's other two modes of armature-supported sculptures are not site specific, they are specifically meant for presentation in a gallery space and, I would argue, for museum acquisition. This is not necessarily the case for the works heretofore discussed.

Within the arrangement of works I term the Engagements, two recurrent, broad forms emerge. These are the ovular, convex forms of the respective series *Mitosis* and *Wishing Stones* and the contracted, curvilinear elements akin to animate spines and rib cages of the *Vertebrae* series. The *Wishing Stones* come late in Unger's practice and are a refinement of the surfaces in the *Mitosis* series. Playful and poignant, the stones are multimodal and demonstrate the return, however brief, of jewel-tone and umber pigments in the sculpture. The series takes its referent from the wave-scrubbed, hand-smoothed pebbles and beach glass Unger became fascinated by on a family trip to the Maine coast.

The concept behind the petrified heart forms and primordial eggs of the *Mitosis* series seems to have taken shape during the 1994–95 period when Unger enjoyed another residency at Yaddo and her second Pollock-Krasner grant. Based in then-recent scientific discoveries evincing the early stages of mammalian development (gametes and zygotes), Unger reached back to lessons and skills honed in graduate school under Niizuma to compress and reduce mythology, science, and material into a deceptively modest, formal abstraction that is both face and egg, both heart and fist. What emerged was a kind

1.23
Mary Ann Unger, *Ode to Tatlin*, 1991 (installation view), painted steel, 19 × 32 × 26 ft. Aaron Copland School of Music, Flushing, Queens.

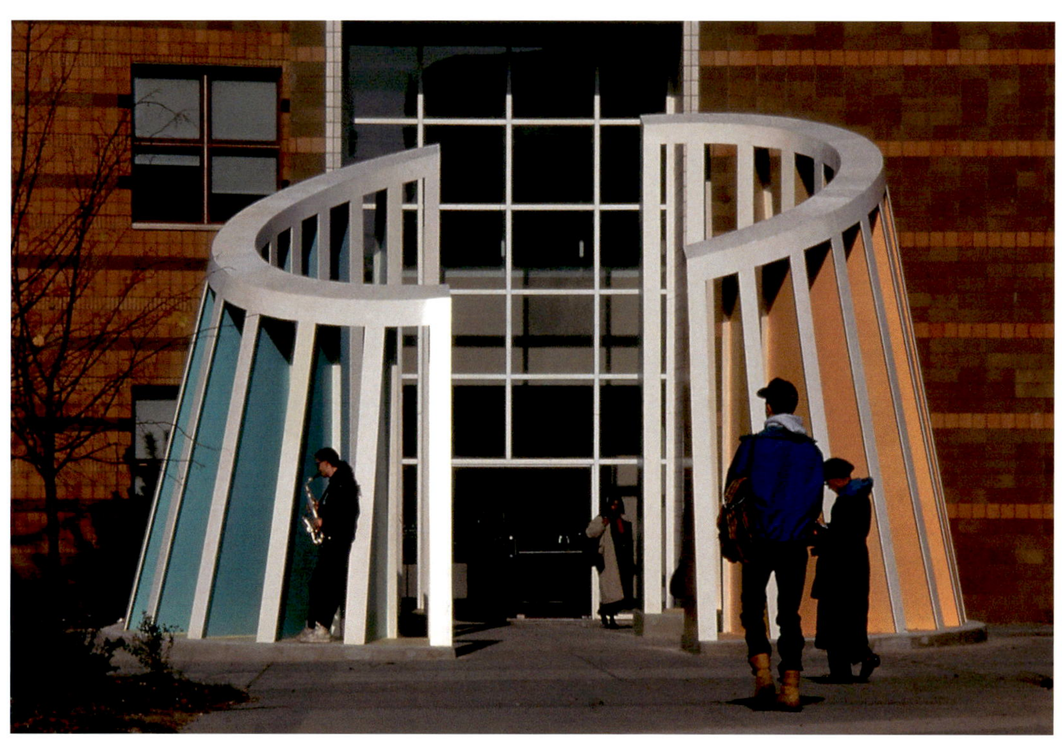

of lunar waxing gibbous form[79]—oblong and partial, with the semblance of being carved from rock, skin, or bone.

By layering cheesecloth over the armature before coating the sculpted forms in Hydrocal, Unger was able to test out the textural interplay between age, wear, repair, damage, and depth without having to use rasps or other burnishing tools. What is so fascinating is that Unger's practice is additive here: the fissures and crevices resulting from a building up of the lip or ridge of plaster, not due to incision marks or carving. The cheesecloth added to the information of the surface, but also added the imposition of textile grid with volume. Like Niizuma, Unger was known for a "sensitive use of textures" and design patterning that ranged "from the geometric to the organic," employing motifs and forms drawn from "folk art, fabrics, and ritual vessels."[80] In many ways, this innovation provides Unger with the theoretical apparatus to consider working in four dimensions: the cheesecloth adds to the surface of the structures an element akin to memory.

Scale does interesting work for Unger in these ovular forms reminiscent of the *ovato rotondo* of the Renaissance depicting the Madonna and Child, which was reanimated in colonial-era portraiture when European families were transatlantically separated from loved ones. Similar to the *Fragments*, the *Mitosis* forms are scaled about the size of a quarter- to half-length bust portrait or, more directly, mirror size. The scale makes these seeming fossilized remains of something supra- or pre-human—a dinosaur, giant, chthonic goddess, titan—oddly prescient. These various diachronic references leverage the formal element of scale to heighten the possibilities of multiple interpretations. Though offering different thematic encounters, structurally, there is much that accords the portrait-size forms with the monumental installation *Across the Bering Strait*. Unger was employing all the same materials, and there is a sense that perhaps she and her assistants were working across the structures, taking what is learned from one and readjusting the admixture or timeline on others.

The works in the *Vertebrae* series come out of Unger's pregnancy and are hand-sanded, jigsaw-cut recitations on the way a body bends and arches to accommodate new life, in bright, sometimes dayglow colors. In their attachment to the wall, and sometimes to the floor, the *Vertebrae* also seem a return to her graphite drawings and white plaster forms of a short-lived series called *The Waterfall Suite* (1977).

Within the forms of this earlier series, concomitant with the beginning of Unger's relationship with Geoffrey Biddle, the flow and sense of carefully constructed distance is now brought into her body in new flourishing. In the *Vertebrae*, for the first time in her practice, it feels as if Unger was discovering the muse within herself by rediscovering and making anew the *Waterfall Suite* forms. For all their pleasure, they are somewhat quiet and enchanting works that warrant close attention, even kneeling to peer inside and underneath them. Resembling Slinkies cascading from a wall, they have a sonic quality as air moves in between the carved and cutaway passages. In *Red Vertebrae* (1980, fig. 1.24) and *Spoon Music* (1980–81), this tonal sensation is echoed by the tonal shift in colors as one changes perspectives in relation to the objects.

And while the *Vertebrae* proper emerge out of plywood via the practice of carving, the "interrelated masses" between substrate and hand "conveying an emotion; a perfect relationship between the mind and the color, light and weight,"[81] there are some exceptions, particularly in the last years of Unger's life. While they are very different in size, I would suggest that *Fishbone (Skeleton)* (1998), *Shanks* (1996–97), and *Spine* (1991) are also related to the Vertebrae series, though imbued with more sombre, perhaps reflective emotions or resignation.

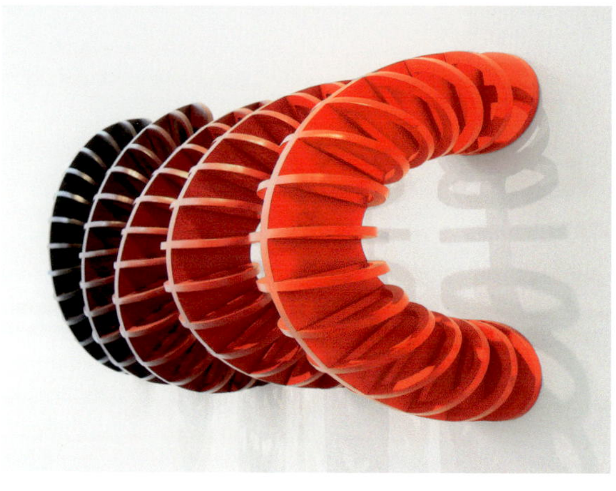

1.24
Mary Ann Unger,
Red Vertebrae, 1980,
painted plywood, 5 units,
(a): 20 × 12 × 15 in.;
(b): 22⅝ × 12 × 14¹¹⁄₁₆ in.;
(c): 26¹⁄₁₆ × 12 × 13⅝ in.;
(d): 28⅜ × 12 × 11⅞ in.;
(e): 30 × 12 × 11⅛ in.
Collection of the
Whitney Museum of
American Art, Gift of
Geoffrey Biddle,
2018.41a–e.

Shanks (fig. 1.25) is an engaged sculptural work of three bow-like, tensile structures enjoined via three mounts (ball-and-socket articulations) to a wall. The work was first displayed in *New Sculptures and Drawings*, Unger's 1997 solo exhibition at the Trans Hudson Gallery in New York. As critic Judith Page asserted at the time, "[*Shanks*] perfectly exemplifies Unger's inclinations—rational yet connected to nature, serene but passionate, rigorously formed yet playful."[82] The vertical structures seem to gently lean into the mounts, lending each of the three individual compounds the appearance of resting against the wall. The tubular, bulbous nodes at the apex of the vertical elements contrast with their slim cylindrical tips, which come to rest just off the floor. This contrast in bulk and sculptural density across the work's expanse provides an animate sense of contrapposto and mediation of shape. The overall effect of the nearly nine-foot, tripartite composition is one of uncanny, restless grace.

The muscular tensile forms echoing the acicular edge of a shiv (homemade knife) and a necessary joint in the leg bone offer a consideration both of the body's ability to harm itself and incur pain from the inside, and of the ways in which a woman's body changes and expands to accommodate new life. The open, spacious composition actively repudiates the solid, blunt masses characteristic of sculpture in the previous generation of the New York School. The expressive modeling of *Shanks'* elements at such a robust scale provides a new model for three-dimensional minimal coherence that rests squarely on representational vocabularies of the figure and belies the short, terse invective of the title (a word used to describe the leg or rib bones of baby animals bred for human consumption). I cannot help but see connections between Unger's streamlined, cuspate gestures and the way Krauss discusses Bourgeois's half forms as "self-immurements" and evocative "part-object-landscapes" that engage embodied experience, bandaging, pleasure, and ambivalence.[83] As in the *Fragments*, Bourgeois again serves as a fantastic counterpoint to Unger; but I am most excited to see Unger's work put in

conversation with the likes of Lygia Clark, Herbert Ferber, Robert Grosvenor, Barbara Hepworth, Jene Highstein, Sherrie Levine, Meera Mukherjee, Robert Morris, Martin Puryear, Joel Shapiro, Alyson Shotz, Simone Leigh, and her dear friend and classmate Ursula von Rydingsvard.[84]

Though critics and curators were fascinated with the Engagements, they were also fighting to find a language both specific and capacious enough to contain intimacy as something both tactile/material and formal. This spills over into the monumental works of the last years of Unger's life, *Misericordia* (1989) and *Across the Bering Strait* (1992–94) being the most well known and, perhaps, the two still extant. In these, the Monuments, Unger's expressive practice dances most freely on the edges of Conceptual and Land Art, yet her sprawling environmental forms maintain their modularity and, thus, their classicism, typographic communication, and formality in a way that is generative and not heavy, overdetermined, or didactic.

Writing for the *New York Times*, Vivien Raynor reviewed *Across the Bering Strait* under the title "Sculptural Works That Defy the Limitations of Definition."[85] Most critics employed a kind of romantic historicism or mythic ecology, characterizing Unger's elongated and increasingly abstract referents to myth and the figure as roots, cholla, teeth, bone, stamen, gauze, saguaro, hands. The scalar amplification of these hard yet organic things has, I think, the opposite effect of the artist's and the critical intention: in calling industrial and bonded-iron forms into ecological conception, the disjunctures read less as playful and more as post-apocalyptic and singular, despite their natural, everyday origins.

Though Unger's structures resemble, or rhyme with, bone, twigs, knives, roots, and other organic networked implements of capacity and conveyance, they are not mimetic. They are autonomous, self-inured implements, sculpting and insisting on a kind of distance that is not critical but mythic and curious, assured if/when approached, hoping for a kind of universality of cultural resonance. Unger constructed and arranged oblique,

1.25
Mary Ann Unger, *Shanks*,
1996–97, Hydrocal and
cheesecloth over steel
armatures, 109 × 98 ×
34 in. Collection of the
Williams College
Museum of Art, Karl E.
Weston Memorial Fund,
M.2020.16.

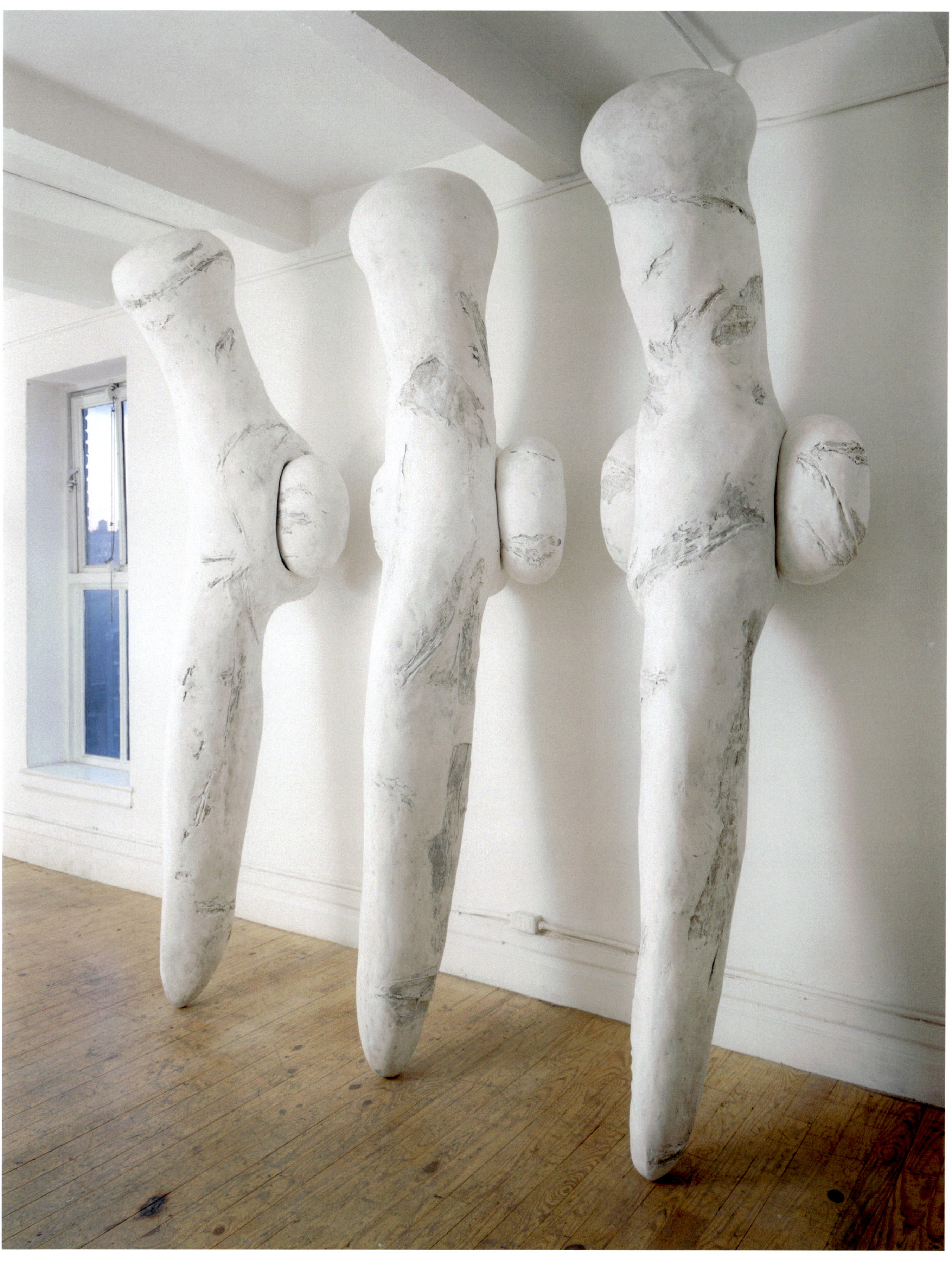

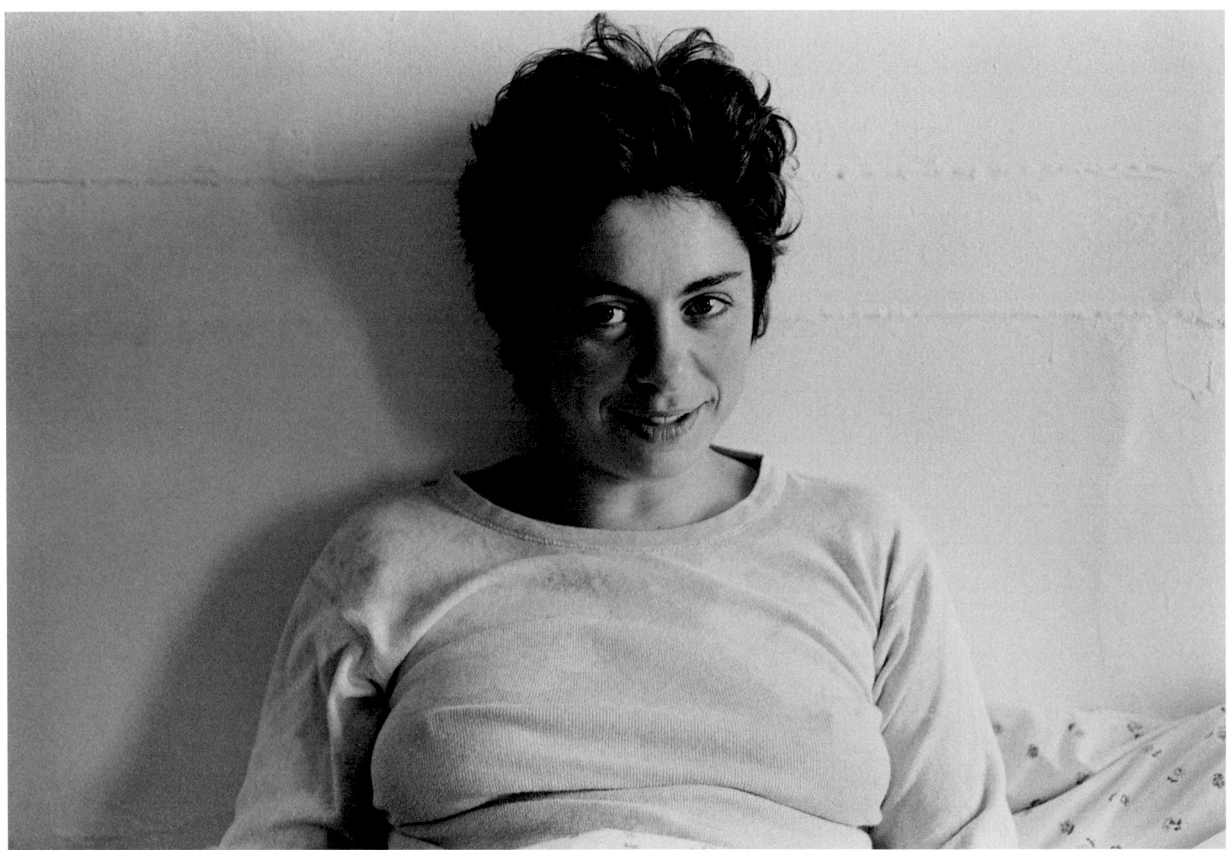

tensile structures as elements—whether on paper on in space—according to the formal qualities of scale, color, and positive/negative space (the space they take up, the space between elements), notched, resting, held together, eliciting emotion and conveying democratic messages of welcome, invitation, and no small amount of awe.

It is toward a mode of giving narrative shape to and providing context for Unger's practice and concerns that this long-form exposition of Unger's life and practice has aimed. As Roberta Smith so deftly articulated in Unger's obituary, as the artist's expressive forms "conjure the body without actually depicting it, these works occupied a territory defined by Eva Hesse and Louise Bourgeois. But the pieces combined a sense of mythic power with a sensitivity to shape that was all their own, achieving subtlety of expression that belied their monumental scale."[86] It is not ours to know why a talent such as Unger's has not yet received the critical considerations, reconsiderations, scholarly papers, surveys, and retrospectives she deserves. But we can, to paraphrase Beyoncé Knowles-Carter, "put some respect on [her] name."

During Mary Ann Unger's life, critics and curators spoke of her work as primordial, mythic, the gothic element of late modernity coming to the fore in a postmodern moment. I think it was futurity Unger was after, the fact that we all return to the earth, all return— through bodily translation or ash—back to the elemental, to regenerate and harbor new life (fig. 1.26). Within the structural possibilities of her verve and vision, Unger's forms manage to be anhydrous in their shadow play: resonant but ineffable acts dark as death, light as hope.

1.26
Mary Ann Unger in her East Third Street loft, New York, 1975. Photo by Geoffrey Biddle. Courtesy of the artist.

Notes

1. Mary Ann Unger, in "Abstraction as a Timeless Art Form," Artists Talk on Art, panel moderated by Clement Meadmore, with John L. Moore, Robert Murray, Peter Stroud, Martin Bull, and Mary Ann Unger, Fulcrum Gallery, SoHo, New York, January 21, 1994. Artists Talk on Art Records, circa 1974–2018, Archives of American Art, Smithsonian Institution.

2. The influential art critic Barbara Rose (1936–2020) reminds us that the terms often used to congeal the generational shifts in the postwar New York art world, including mentorship and the lineage and refinement of ideas, largely float above the actual attentions of the artists these terms hope to capture. "Abstract expressionism never existed," Rose recalled in a 2015 interview. "It [as a label] didn't fit anybody.… It [the scene] was the New York School, which includes de Kooning's gestural side, the Newman Color Field side and then Reinhardt's push toward the monochrome." What made this sense of coherence possible, Rose contends, for these individuals with disparate approaches to painterly gestures, materials, and ideals was their proximity to one another in their living, in their social lives, in their age, and largely, but not totally, in their race and gender. Rose, married to Frank Stella at the time, was at the center of the mapped web of bars, studios, galleries, parks, cold-water flats, and jazz haunts where the scene coalesced. See William S. Smith, "More Is Less," *Art News*, December 28, 2020, http://www.artnews.com/art-in-america /interviews/barbara-rose-abc-art-1234580339/, which reprints the interview with Barbara Rose first published in October 2015.

3. Mary Ann Unger, Guggenheim Fellowship Statement, 1992, 1.

4. Unger, Guggenheim Fellowship Statement, 1.

5. Unger, Guggenheim Fellowship Statement, 1.

6. Roberta Smith, "Mary Ann Unger, 53, a Noted Sculptor and Curator, Is Dead," Obituaries, *New York Times*, January 3, 1999; drawing from Unger's 1992 Guggenheim Fellowship statement.

7. Sara C. Beasley, "Leonard DeLonga: Artist-Teacher-Bodhisattva," http://www.buddhistdoor.net /features/leonard-delonga-artist-teacher -bodhisattva.

8. In honor of the DeLongas, Mary Ann Unger's parents, Dorothy and William Unger, made a gift of Unger's pigmented plaster, framed sculpture *Pittsburgh Landscape* (1982–83) to the Mount Holyoke College Art Museum in 1994. It remains one of the earliest extant sculptural works in Unger's hand.

9. See Shannon Collins Pan, *DeLonga: A Pictorial Look at the Art of Leonard DeLonga* (Blurb Books, 2009), 104–6.

10. Unger, Guggenheim Fellowship Statement, 1.

11. I love this beautiful and evocative line from Margaret Kross's exhibition review and interview with ektor garcia in *Artforum* and find such connective tissue between garcia's and Unger's practices, though birthed from different concerns and temporal spaces. See Margaret Kross, "Openings: ektor garcia," *Artforum*, September 2019, http://www.artforum.com/print/201907 /margaret-kross-on-ektor-garcia-80524.

12. Unger, in "Abstraction as a Timeless Art Form."

13. Special thanks to the archivist of the Mount Holyoke Archives and Special Collections for pointing me to the listing of honorary degree recipients of the college since 1926. In hindsight, one could trace to these early yet formative years in Hadley, Massachusetts, Unger's aggregation of a singular if flexible typography of structural glyphs and references, rich in contrasts and dismissive of material hierarchies but grounded in elastic, expressive, and exaggerated forms. Throughout her studies, the fields of anthropology, literature, art, and political economy were deeply in flux due to the flood of continental philosophy being translated into English for the first time and the renewed possibility for freer travel after the war. In a moment of individual exploration, the collective agency and activism of one's peers and broad cultural change made the personal deeply political, particularly with regard to self-presentation and resistance to certain gendered notions of what a Mount Holyoke woman "should" be. While Unger graduated a year before the historic spring and fall semesters of 1968—when the college either amended or overturned decades-old rules ("parietals") governing who could have a car on campus, restricting smoking and drinking in the dorms, and regulating when male visitors were permitted in the dorms—Unger's class had begun to press upon the outmoded regulations of the dress code and mentored younger students in community organizing and political actions.

14. Unger, Guggenheim Fellowship Statement, 1; Geoffrey Biddle, email correspondence with the author, April 12, 2021.

15. Barbara Hepworth, *Barbara Hepworth: Carvings and Drawings*, with an introduction by Herbert Read (London: Lund Humphries, 1952), 8.

16. Unger came to California at the precise moment that Judy Chicago began teaching the first women's art history course at the California State University, Fresno (then Fresno State College). She may have followed a boyfriend to California, but she stayed on her own terms, exploring whether graduate study was something she wanted to invest in.

17. Perhaps most famous of these instances is the series of sessions and readings staged by Ntozake Shange and her collaborator, Paula Moss, from

1972 to 1974, which would become the series of twenty monologues in the choreopoem *for colored girls / who have considered suicide when the rainbow / is enuf* (1975).

18. J. P. Hodin, *Barbara Hepworth* (New York: David McKay, 1961), 23–24.

19. Hepworth, "Artists in Society," in *Barbara Hepworth: Carvings and Drawings*, 11.

20. Rosalind Krauss, *Perpetual Inventory* (Cambridge, MA: MIT Press, 2010).

21. Unger, Guggenheim Fellowship Statement, 1.

22. Barbara Hepworth, "Approach to Sculpture," *The Studio* 132, no. 643 (October 1946): accessed online.

23. Hepworth, *Barbara Hepworth: Carvings and Drawings*, 11.

24. Unger, Guggenheim Fellowship Statement, 1.

25. Unger, Guggenheim Fellowship Statement, 1.

26. Unger, Guggenheim Fellowship Statement, 1.

27. Ruth Asawa, cited in "The Art of Space: Ruth Asawa's Sculptural Installations," in *The Sculpture of Ruth Asawa: Contours in the Air*, ed. Timothy Anglin Burgland and Daniell Cornell (Berkeley: University of California Press, 2006), 138.

28. Early readers of the 1962 English translation of Heidegger's *Sein und Zeit* (1927) by John Macquarrie and Edward Robinson were discussing *affect* as a kind of recomposition or reorientation of mood, which impinges upon Sartre's sense of the artistic situation. One can imagine the white wall, high gloss of a Donald Judd or the downtown, dimly-lit rough cement ground on which a Richard Nonas is poised and imagine the encounter eliciting a Mark Rothko–like effect on the senses and the emotions of the viewer.

29. Linda B. Shearer, the former director of the Williams College Museum of Art from 1989 to 2004, was in the curatorial department at the Guggenheim from 1969 to 1980, where she had a key hand in assisting or organizing all of the presentations I have listed. (We chatted on the phone once and she was magnificent and generous.) I am grateful to Ben N. Ward, Williams '22, who served as my curatorial research intern during academic year 2020–21 and compiled copious lists of every exhibition presented at the Jewish Museum and the Guggenheim during the 1972 to 1975 seasons. I do not mean to suggest that only sculpture presentations sustained Unger's attention during these years. I believe Unger would be the first to say that an artist learns by attending to the work of other artists, regardless of medium. But sculpture does offer a way of narrowing down the options in "the city of museums," as it allows us to pinpoint the artists and shows her faculty, friends, and her peers would expect her to see and/or be able to speak to.

30. Documentary evidence suggests that while not included in the billing, the artist Richard Nonas (born 1936) may also have had a work included in the show. See Peter Moore, archival installation views for the exhibition *5 Sculptors—7,000 Sq. Feet*, June 10–24, 1972, MoMA PS1 Archives, III.B.108, the Museum of Modern Art Archives, New York, INPS1.3.7, http://www.moma.org/calendar /exhibitions/3938?installation_image_index=4.

31. Avram Kampf, *Luise Kaish: Sculpture* (New York: Jewish Museum, 1973), 3.

32. One cannot help but wonder how Unger's practice would have been influenced had she studied with Kaish, who became professor of visual arts and chair of painting and sculpture at Columbia in 1980 and retired in 1986.

33. John Russell, "Art That Tells of the Jewish Experience," *New York Times*, October 24, 1975.

34. Roberta Smith, "George Sugarman, a Sculptor of Colorful Works, Dies at 87," Obituaries, *New York Times*, August 31, 1999, http://www.nytimes.com /1999/08/31/arts/george-sugarman-a-sculptor-of -colorful-works-dies-at-87.html.

35. I am thankful here for Ken Johnson's 1999 review of Bladen's end-of-the-century retrospective at MoMA PS1: Ken Johnson, "A Romantic Pushes Minimalism to the Maximum," *New York Times*, February 19, 1999, http://www.nytimes.com /1999/02/19/arts/art-review-a-romantic-pushes -minimalism-to-the-maximum.html.

36. There is an interesting temporal resonance between Sugarman's pedestal-free works and the works of Mark di Suvero, Anthony Caro, Donald Judd, and even the sans-stretcher extended paintings of Lynda Benglis and Sam Gilliam.

37. Drawings aside, Sugarman's influence on Unger is most apparent in her *Vertebrae* series (1980) of slinky-like, engaged sculptures formed of plywood and bright, sometimes dayglow pigments.

38. George Sugarman, artist's website, accessed December 2, 2021, https://georgesugarman.com.

39. Rosalind Krauss, "Louise Bourgeois: Portrait of the Artist as Fillete," in *Bachelors* (Cambridge, MA: MIT Press, 1999), 54. I specifically use Krauss here so as to return to her later and make both a formal and rhetorical connection to Unger's *Fragments* series and their impetus.

40. Unger, Guggenheim Fellowship Statement, 2. Due to their bulk, and Unger's early rejection of working in series, all her early molds were discarded. See Mary Ann Unger, in "Systematic/ Metrical Patterning: In-Town and Out-of-Town," Artists Talk on Art, panel moderated by George Woodman, with Gloria Klein, Tony Robbin, Mary Ann Unger, Charles DiJulio, Richard Kallweit, and Clark Richert (from Criss-Cross Artist Co-op in Boulder, Colorado), Landmark Gallery, New York, January 11, 1980. Artists Talk on Art Records,

Ballard

circa 1974–2018, Archives of American Art, Smithsonian Institution.

41. In New York, Niizuma moved through an international milieu of Japanese and European émigrés who found the city (and Southern California) hospitable to their need for community and also reinvention in the decades following WWII. Though not a member of the Fluxus mélange, Niizuma was a gifted photographer as well as a sculptor. Close friends with Yoko Ono, Niizuma served as unofficial archivist and chronicler of Ono's actions and performances in the mid to late 1960s, infamously being the first person to cut a snippet of Ono's clothing in the 1964 performance *Cut Piece* at the Museum of Modern Art.

42. Grace Glueck, "Sculptures Come Out 'Into Environment,'" August 4, 1971, *New York Times*, 38.

43. Owen Sindorf, "Reflections on Robert Sindorf," Prezi presentation, accessed April 14, 2021, http://prezi.com/7-rmrfpvsmb9/robert-sindorf/?frame=13cb9f058cc6aee7c56a2752d7782faa280373bb.

44. In May 2019, I was at the Archives of American Art looking through the curatorial files and personal correspondence of Dorothy Canning Miller (1904–2003), the eminent curator of paintings and sculpture at the Museum of Modern Art, New York, for more than thirty years. From 1971 to 1973, Miller had multiple written exchanges with Minoru Niizuma regarding various potential commissions and projects. The line "to shape the moon from bone," from which the present exhibition derives its title, is my memory of the wording of a quote I recall reading in one of their letters. I believe it is actually a meta-memory: Miller writing to Niizuma about her love of his practice and recalling to mind (and to the page) a previous conversation with Niizuma, months earlier, in which the artist uttered these lines as a metaphor for his impetus to *make*. In her letter, Miller reminds Niizuma of how the powerful phrase has stuck with her months later. The phrase has also stuck with me. The Unger exhibition title, then, is adapted from my memory of Miller's memory of Niizuma's words. Sadly, due to COVID-19 protocols at the moment this catalogue went to press, I cannot access these undigitized archives to find the exact language. However, I like the poetics of this, and the line beautifully accords with how I feel about Unger's work and creates an evocative bridge between her and Niizuma.

45. Geoffrey Biddle, *Rock In A Landslide*, e-publication, 2020, http://www.geoffreybiddle.com/rock-in-a-landslide.

46. Via email thread between Allison Kaufman (director, Mary Ann Unger Estate), Eve Biddle, Geoffrey Biddle, and Horace Ballard, May 13, 2021, Kaufman and Geoffrey Biddle shared the names of the other artist-residents of the Third Avenue building, which turned into an artist-owned co-op

during Unger's last years. At the time of this writing, past and current residents included Cecile Abish, Walter Abish, Howard Guttenplan, Eileen Hickey-Hulme, John Hulme, Semadar Megged, Natan Nuchi, Theodora Skipitares, Carol Yoshimura, and Fumio Yoshimura.

47. Louise McCagg, entry for Mary Ann Unger in the "Exhibitions" section, *Craft Horizons* 37, no. 5 (October 1977): 49. It may or may not be of interest that Hastings's work is not mentioned.

48. Founded by Ivan Karp after he left the Leo Castelli Gallery in 1969.

49. Rebecca Skafsgaard Lowery, "Criss-Cross and the Gender of Pattern-Making," in *With Pleasure: Pattern and Decoration in American Art: 1972–1985*, ed. Ann Lowery (New Haven: Yale University Press, 2019), 112.

50. Lowery, *With Pleasure*, 112.

51. Unger, in "Systematic/Metrical Patterning."

52. Unger, in "Systematic/Metrical Patterning."

53. Biddle, *Rock In A Landslide*.

54. Katy Hessel, in conversation with "Frida Kahlo" and "Käthe Kollwitz" of the Guerrilla Girls, *The Great Women Artists*, podcast, October 27, 2020, 5:09–6:43 of 48:03, http://open.spotify.com/episode/2zlRgyq7eIpNLgtK7p4ftq?si=TNT7SRY0SPWTJZsWGpWbnA&utm_source=sms&dl_branch=1.

55. Katy Hessel, *Great Women Artists*, 12:30–14:05.

56. Biddle, *Rock In A Landslide*. I am equally grateful to my colleague Lisa Dorin for helping me think through these critical alignments and alliances between heart and expectation held and faced by so many women.

57. Though as yet unconfirmed, it is possible that Unger may also have had a hand in shaping (if not, having work shown in) the now-legendary Guerrilla Girls–curated exhibition of over one hundred female and femme-expressing artists, *The Night the Palladium Apologized*, in October 1985. She is not listed on the poster, but the poster is clear about the list of participants being incomplete.

58. Michael Brenson, "Art: Sculpture, 'Figure as Image of the Psyche,'" *New York Times*, November 8, 1985.

59. Michael Brenson, "Art: Sculpture."

60. Michael Brenson, "Art: Jasper Johns Prints on Show at the Modern," *New York Times*, May 23, 1986.

61. Brenson, "Art: Jasper Johns Prints."

62. In Unger's sketchbooks-cum-journals from the early 1990s, we begin to see her think through what she calls "the Mary problem," which, to my best sense, is how to find new ways of rendering the triangular sacred form of Mary holding an infant or crucified Christ into a unique but equally resonant shape. In her "working it out" via drawing and shade, the arms of Mary and her mantle become extended and beam-like. See also Smith, "Mary Ann Unger, 53."

63. Biddle, *Rock In A Landslide*.

64. Aria Dean and Cory John Scozzari, "Review: Aria Dean: *Studio Parasite*," Instagram post, @lol_prosciutto, February 22, 2021.

65. During her life, Unger used the word *modules* as in "the modules / the modularities" of my practice. For posthumous synthesis and flow, I find the terms *arrangements* or *modes* equally helpful, but would discourage any sense of strict categorization, grouping, or segmenting.

66. Today, the terms abstraction and conceptual art are more capaciously used than Unger knew them to be. As Charles Gaines reminds us, "Conceptualism of the 1960s and 1970s was based on the idea of interrogating the possibilities of a work of art through an investigation of the structure of the [work] itself." The analytical language of "involute patterning based on systemic and mathematical algorithms, arbitrary but precise" marked, for Unger and the Criss-Cross artists, the formal instantiation of a third way between minimal sheen and charismatic Abstract Expressionism. (A "fourth way" might be something like Bourgeois—an automatism that, interestingly, does not seem to interest Unger, who finds power in the personal-expressive vein, but I digress.) Early analytical and systemic or conceptual practice offered (via the media of an expressive vein in the midst of abstractive ideas) the possibility of a dimensional art object that was relational rather than spatially bounded. For example, rich pattering becoming the "trace" of an idea, standing in for the fully wrought work meant to be experienced/felt internally. Artists like Howardena Pindell and Sol LeWitt would take this one step further (and into high conceptualism) when the analytical tools and numerical markers of patterns in themselves began to constitute the formal language in their work. See Charles Gaines, "Negotiating Abstraction," originally published in *Howardena Pindell: What Remains to Be Seen*, ed. Naomi Beckwith and Valerie Cassel Oliver (New York: Prestel, 2018), http://pindell.mcachicago.org/essays/howardena-pindell-negotiating-abstraction/.

67. I am grateful to the Davidson Gallery for their enduring generosity and fellowship. During the research for this exhibition, it became clear why artists like Torkwase Dyson, Sam Messenger, and Mary Ann Unger would find representation with the Davidsons during their careers. The inestimable Dyson shared in a recent Instagram post, "I've made hundreds and hundreds of drawings trying to get someplace… the ability of the human brain and soul to use physics/engineering and body memory to create something that makes you feel wonder. [The relationship between drawing and sculpture] is not magic and it's not directly referential, it's a visual equation… both determinable/measurable and absolutely unmeasurable." Torkwase Dyson, @torkwasedyson, April 7, 2021. I could see Unger and Messenger uttering similar connections.

68. The similarities between Unger's exercises and those originated by Josef Albers suggest Unger may have absorbed this form of engagement from the Black Mountain alumni working and teaching in New York during her formative years (possibly even Clark Richert via Buckminster Fuller).

69. *Guernica* returned to Spain in 1981.

70. Krauss, "Louise Bourgeois," 54. Though published in *Bachelors* in 1999, Krauss's original essay on Bourgeois was published ten years earlier, in 1989, making it probable that Unger would have heard about it and intuited its profound resonance, if not read it directly.

71. Alice Neel, from her diaries in the 1940s, quoted in Phoebe Hoban's *Alice Neel: The Art of Not Sitting Pretty* (New York: St. Martin's, 2010), 140.

72. I cannot resist noting the coincidence that during the Lillehammer Olympics in 1994, Munch's *The Scream* was stolen from the National Gallery in Oslo, to be found and returned four months later, after considerable international press and intrigue. It is fascinating to contemplate how this famous work of modernism, its photograph circulating and disseminated throughout the globe during this period of restless anxiety in Unger's life and practice, may have found analogy with the *Fragments*.

73. Unger, in "Systematic/Metrical Patterning."

74. Unger, in "Systematic/Metrical Patterning."

75. Unger, in "Abstraction as a Timeless Art Form."

76. In addition to the public artworks discussed, there are six others: *Pineapple* (1990), at North Regional Courthouse, Ft. Lauderdale, Florida; *Gazebo* (1989), at Merrimack Riverfront Park, Lawrence, Massachusetts; *Tower* (1989), at Cave Creek Sports Complex, Phoenix, Arizona; *Wave* (1989, see fig. 2.5), at City Hall Plaza, Tampa, Florida; *Muktesvara Arch* (1987), at Gaithersburg Regional Library, Gaithersburg, Maryland; and *Forrestal Garden* (1987), at Princeton Forrestal Village, Princeton, New Jersey.

77. Michael Brenson, "Weekend: Mary Ann Unger, Tweed Garden," *New York Times*, December 6, 1985.

78. There is also, in *Ode to Tatlin*, a hint of old wooden roller-coaster supports as the music, of course, is moving, and the clefs are not static. Very cool!

79. Again, there are no 1:1 correlations in Unger's work, but there are analogies, resonances, and layerings from history and culture. One such nod to form is that in January 25, 1994, the joint space project

Clementine (aka the Deep Space Program Science Experiment, or DSPSE) between NASA and the Strategic Defense Initiative Organization launched; a few months later, it was already sending pictures back to Earth, and global news outlets printed the images of the "dark side" of the lunar surface, surrounded by a solar corona and Venus.

80. Roberta Smith, "Minoru Niizuma, 67, Sculptor and Teacher," Obituaries, *New York Times*, September 29, 1998.

81. Barbara Hepworth, *Unit 1: The Modern Movement in English Architecture, Painting and Sculpture*, ed. Herbert Read (London: Cassell, 1934), 19.

82. It is also interesting that Judith Page's review of Unger's 1997 solo presentation in *Sculpture Magazine* is printed in the same issue as important career-defining reviews of solo presentations by Beverly Pepper and Mel Edwards— multidisciplinary artists whose respective finesse with extended media accords with Unger's interests and skill. It is impossible not to consider how formidable Unger's instincts were, and how well positioned she was in the critical discourse of the art world just prior to her death.

83. Rosalind Krauss, "Louise Bourgeois: Portrait of the Artist as Fillette," *Bachelors* (Cambridge, MA: MIT Press, 2000), 68.

84. To my eye, Clark's, Ferber's, and von Rydingsvard's work perhaps most fluently spoke with Unger's at the moment of its making. Today, the work of ektor garcia comes to mind.

85. Raynor's review gives the earliest articulation of how *Across the Bering Strait* was presented. "At Trans Hudson, [Mary Ann Unger]'s installation titled *Across the Bering Strait* lies low, illuminated by a couple of lights on the floor. The illusion is of an exercise in multiple shadows overlapping one another on the walls and floor; the reality is a crowd of shapes that are phallic, visceral and even sausage-like. They lie as if thrown on stubby supports cleft like catapults." Unger and the Trans Hudson Gallery in Jersey City share the review with work by Tom Doyle and Elaine Lorenz at the Quietude Gallery, in East Brunswick, New York. See Vivien Raynor, "Sculptural Works That Defy the Limitations of Definition (review)," *New York Times*, May 29, 1994.

86. Smith, "Mary Ann Unger, 53."

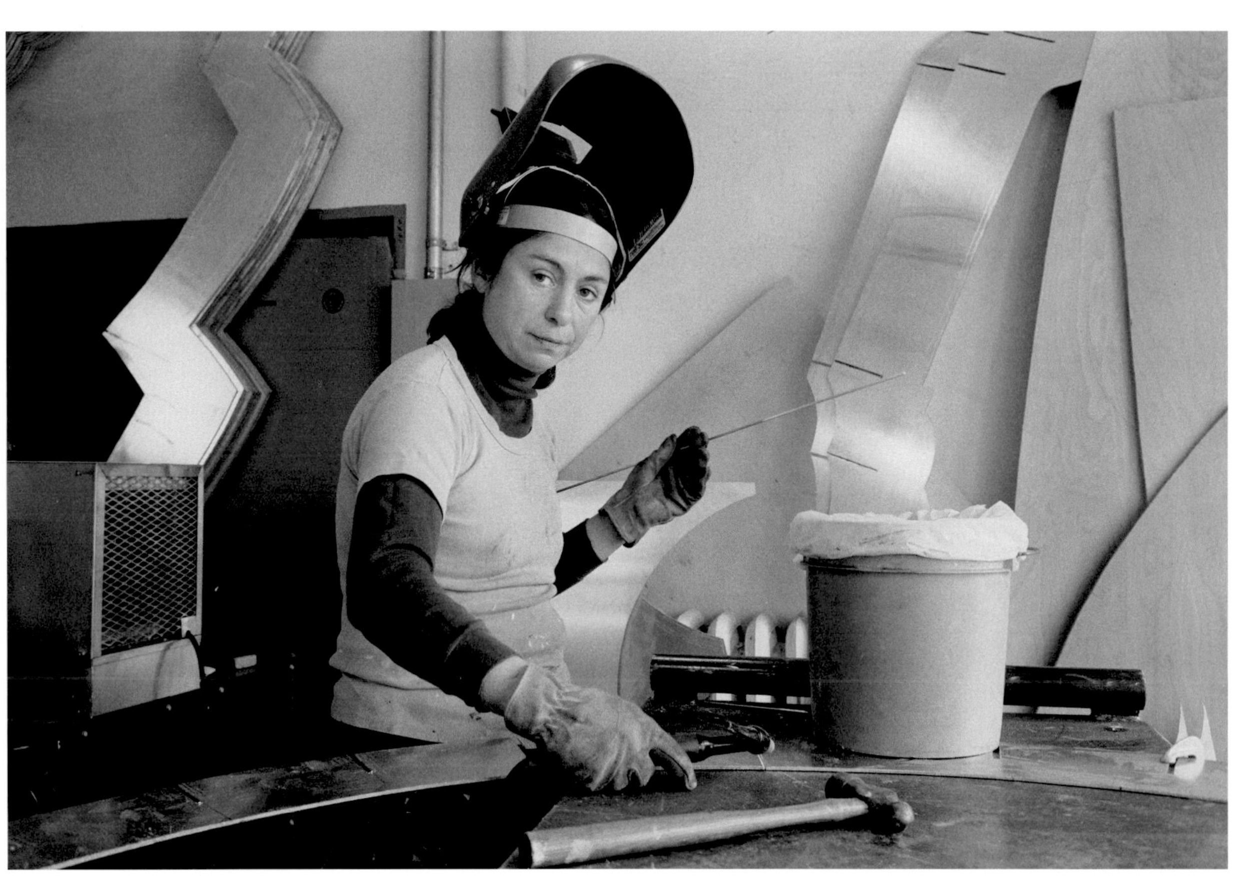

Gathering
A Roundtable Conversation

Horace D. Ballard,
Eve Biddle, and
Sarah Montross

The following conversation took place via Zoom on May 19, 2021.

Horace D. Ballard I could not think of two more exciting people to be in conversation with around Mary Ann Unger's life and legacy than Eve Biddle, artist, curator, and cofounder and codirector of the Wassaic Project, and Sarah Montross, senior curator at deCordova Sculpture Park and Museum.

Eve is Unger's daughter and cofounded the Mary Ann Unger Estate with her father, the photographer Geoffrey Biddle, about twelve years ago. Sarah is a curator and scholar who thinks deeply about the possibilities, extensions, and resonance of artists working in multiple dimensions encompassing sited work and installation.

Thank you, Eve, for joining me in conversation today and consistently over the past three years. And thank you, Sarah, for your keen interest in Mary Ann's practice.

Eve Biddle I'm really happy we're doing this, and I'm really happy you're here, Sarah.

Sarah Montross So am I! Thank you for having me.

Horace Eve, when you think about your memories of your mother, especially those particular memories of her at work in her studio at the loft (fig. 2.1), what comes to mind? What are you hearing, what are you smelling, what are you seeing?

Eve As a student at Williams College, I took a sculpture class with Amy Podmore. There are oxy-acetylene welders down in the sculpture shop at Williams and I thought, "God, this smells so good, why does it smell so good?" And part of it is that Mom had an oxy-acetylene welder in her studio end of the loft. I grew up in this 1,800-square-foot loft in the East Village, and about a third of the floor was Mom's studio. We would eat lunch together with Dad when I was a kid. Dad would come out of the darkroom smelling like chemicals, and Mom would come out of the studio smelling like an oxy-acetylene welder.

She had these black turtlenecks with little polka-dotted holes all over them from the sparks, and that oxy-acetylene burn smells like Mom and home. It's just really familiar in a really nice way. I also remember her hands were rough from working with all these different materials. Her hands were super strong and super rough in a nice way, in a scratch-your-back kind of way… You know, the work was just a part of our lives. It was in the house, in the conversation, in the mix. That way of looking and talking about what people were working on was fun. It was in the mix all the time. We lived with their art, and with other peoples' art.

Dad's been revisiting his contact sheets since the mid-1970s as he's working on the book *Rock In A Landslide*. It started out as a graduation present to me, and it has grown into a book about him and Mom. He's been pulling images of me and Mom and work and our home, and we're just in it (fig. 2.2). I mean, there I am at seven years old, helping to mix up plaster (fig. 2.3), or sitting around in a diaper with a bottle in a chair in the studio.

Sarah So, the studio was right there, in the apartment where you lived?

Eve It's the same floor. We had the entire eighth floor as a loft in this Bowery building off Third Avenue, which is now the Estate. It was part of Cooper Union Community Board / AIR placements. We rented directly from New York City, and eventually we bought the building from the city with the other artists in the building, and a lot of the original artists in the building are still there.

Dad's darkroom was in the apartment; Mom's studio was in the apartment. She had a clean office and then the dirty space. She also had a barn upstate. She was in real estate to make a living for a while, and she was the broker in a big deal in 1984. They bought a house in Ulster County and built a little barn up there. They actually bought a property with a barn, and two months after they bought the house, the barn fell down! So, they built a new barn, and she had work space and fabrication space also. But most of the work got built in the city, on the eighth floor of this building, which is kind of crazy.

Sarah How did the work get out of the building?

Eve It's an old industrial building. By the time Horace first visited the estate in 2018, and, in fact, as of ten years ago, there's a regular push-button elevator. But the elevator shaft is ten feet by ten feet. I remember it was originally an industrial, hand-operated elevator with no auto return. We knew everyone in the building, because between 8 a.m. and 11 p.m.,

you had to respond to the elevator buzzer. You had to stick your head out the door into the shaft and yell, "What floor are you on?" And if you closed the elevator doors in your apartment, you couldn't get them back open, you'd have to go to the floor above and jump down into the elevator and open the doors from the inside. If you dropped your keys down the elevator shaft, you'd have to bring the elevator down to the basement, then up four feet from the bottom to get them. You really wanted to get it right. It was great fun. I loved operating the hand-crank elevator. And there was an opening at the top, so for some of Mom's twelve-, sixteen-foot-long pieces of *Across the Bering Strait*, you could bring them into the elevator and go up and get down to the ground level fine. But now (with the push-button elevator), the pieces we reinstalled at the estate, we had to bring up the stairs!

Sarah The conversations I have with artists working at scale often include concerns like, "Oh, I made this piece, how do I get it out of my building?" or "How do I break it down and reassemble it?" The tricks of armature, and the building in of those tricks into the piece and its travel, I think, are so interesting.

Eve Yes. And Mom didn't need to do that. We had this amazing, amazing space.

Horace Eve, I wonder if you could say more about one of these large-scale works,

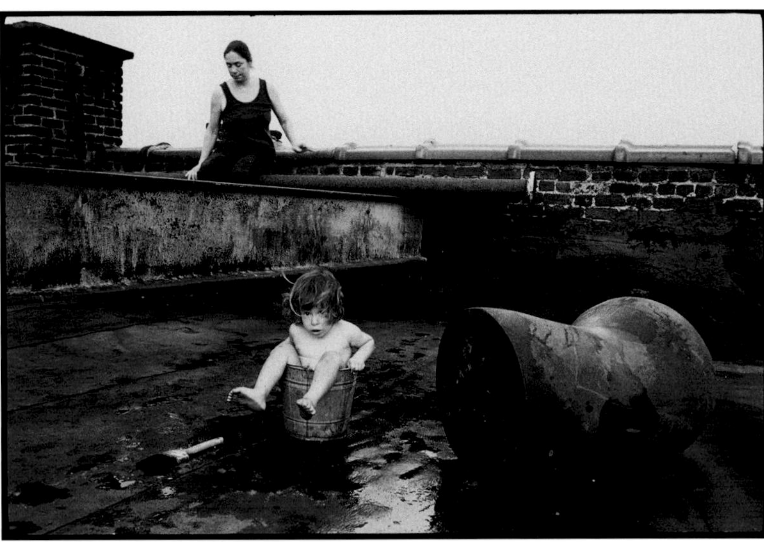

2.2
Eve Biddle and Mary Ann Unger on the roof, Third Street, New York, 1984. Photo by Geoffrey Biddle. Courtesy of the artist.

Ballard, Biddle, Montross

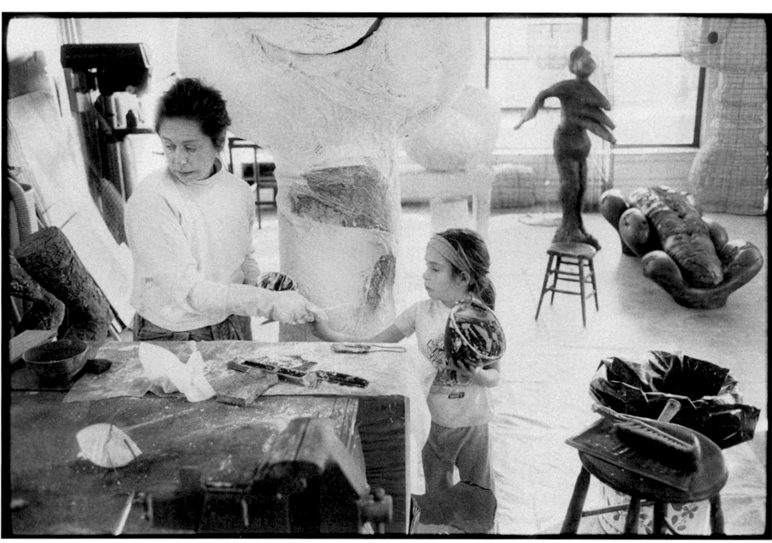

specifically the work the Williams College Museum of Art (WCMA) recently acquired, *Shanks* (1996–97, see fig. 1.25). When members of the museum staff and our Visiting Committee and Fellows visited the estate just weeks before the pandemic shutdown in winter 2020, you generously discussed the facture and the surface of the work and just how close to the eye and the hand that armature is. Could you say more about how Unger created a piece like *Shanks* or those elements of *Across the Bering Strait* composed of steel-rod armature and Hydrocal?

Eve   Mom came from a family of engineers. Her dad and her brother both went to the Massachusetts Institute of Technology, and she entered Mount Holyoke as a biochemistry major. She joked that she would sit in the science lab watching people go by in their painty overalls, and she would break test tubes all afternoon! So, she switched to being an art major but carried over this math and chemistry underpinning. She was always a strong mathematician; you can see it so clearly in her drawing, and she's an incredible draftsperson. She instilled a love of math in me, and she had a real clarity of vision around her expertise about surface creation and structure.

In a piece like *Shanks*, there's a lot going on. The three bases are anchored to the wall with a simple bracket. The long, vertical pieces lean into the brackets. There's nothing holding them together—they're just leaning—but they fit beautifully. And they fit in a way that's really stable. How do you get to that stable, elegant stasis? When she was welding the steel armature, there was some room for improvisation but not a lot, because you don't want the armature to be ponderous. She wasn't getting it 3D printed; that wasn't a technology that was available. There were no CNC routers. She had a vision of what the shape would be and how it would function in terms of its balance. And she was able to go from that idea in her head to an armature that was very close to how it would be on the wall.

Shanks is one of her few white pieces. The surface that you see, that finish, is bonelike or stonelike in its nature. And it's pretty thin. She would build the steel armature, totally hollow except for a few reinforced rods, and the gridding is two inches square: an organically shaped, dimensional grid. Then she'd take lengths of cheesecloth, dip them in Hydrocal, and wrap the structure. On top of that, she'd apply more Hydrocal in liquid form, building up the surface. At the very end, there might be some light and very fine reductive work on the top with a rasping file or sandpaper.

Some people have implied there are references to scarification in the work due to this burnishing, but to me, that idea implies a violence or labored, incisive, and reductive work. When Hydrocal hardens, if you try to break that away, you would chip it, so it's not how these forms were made. Anything that is globular or fleshlike, that's all additive. There's this gentleness and care to the way the work was made, even if the result is in some ways referential to scarring or a wound. The process to get there is a much more loving touch. There's no chiseling. It's all this shaping with the hands and the body to get to that surface that references both tenderness and violence. The result is this mysterious organic form composed through this linear process with steps along the way. It's been interesting to unpack that with people visiting the estate and looking at the work because the forms feel so organic, but the process is intentional. Of course, it is reactive in a certain way—there was definitely spontaneity at moments—but the form and the process are deeply structured, which, I think, speaks to that grounding in engineering and mathematics.

Sarah What you just shared is pinging so many ideas. I'm thinking of the sculptor Kathy Butterly, who makes these tiny ceramics, but she describes when she's making her vessels and using her sculpting tools as equivalent to the careful touch you'd take to brush someone's hair, soft-like. Butterly's distorting and carving and making pieces and adding up and so forth may be similar to what you're describing. I like this idea that in a portion of Mary Ann Unger's process, there's almost this loving petting, but as an engineered, attentive gesture.

Also, I was curious as you were talking: some of the works I know are these allusions to bodily forms, like to vertebrae. How much did it matter that some of these works are larger, or just slightly larger, than the body? Did it matter to your mother that the limits of a female body were expressed oversize? Was that conscious in her mind? In the current moment, some female sculptors, in particular, talk about these relationships—that they wanted to be sculptors, in part, because they wanted to do it themselves. There's a kind of self-resilience: "I want to do it myself, I want to make it myself, and I want to be able to make it within the bounds of my capacity but just a little larger than life too." Did Unger express these ideas?

Eve That's all really interesting, and gender is an interesting dynamic. A lot of what Mom made walked that line between engineered and organic, male and female, monumental scale and intimate form, things looking like they might be fleshy but being hard, being big but fragile.

Mom was kind of macho in a certain way—in an exciting way. It's interesting: you talk about "making it yourself." We have encountered men who knew her work when she was alive and worked with her and still don't believe that she made it herself. Like, really? You knew her! You saw the apartment! We have ample photographic evidence. Of course, she had amazing assistants and had a great dialogue with them, and there were some works that went to fabricators to get made. But the biggest stuff, even some of the big public pieces, she made herself, in our home. There was an economy of saving money to make it yourself, but with these Hydrocal pieces, her hand was so important. In the steps where assistants would come in, it was not design; it was not finishing.

Mom talked about being a feminist, and she was a Guerrilla Girl, and she instilled that feminism in me. But she didn't really talk about that idea of proving yourself. That may have been part of what she was thinking about, but it was just being and living, you know? It was sexual and powerful and it was a space where she was owning her power and her sexuality and her machismo and putting it all out there, saying, "Okay, these are going to exist at the same time, deal with it."

Horace Thank you, Eve, for that generous response and thank you, Sarah, for that question. I think, in many ways, I've been trying to frame that question around various forms, modes, and positionings within feminism and Unger's multiple identities for quite some time. Her ability to be herself always, even in the midst of the male-dominated New York art scene of Minimalist sculpture; of taking an idea worked out in one form and transcribing it into another material at a new scalar reality but retaining lightness and crispness of edge in the process of adding mass and volume… The power of her mark and her cognitive act, and the impressive presence the work exudes and enacts in space after such a transcription… It is what draws me to her practice so forcibly and keeps me looking.

In some ways, this last exchange opens up the possibility of thinking about material futures. I'm thinking about the placement of the large-scale works as they exist in collections, and also for institutions that may wish to collaborate with the estate to refabricate, cast, and site—either permanently or semipermanently—works by Unger back into the landscape. Are there other materials that would keep Unger's forceful vision, but

Ballard, Biddle, Montross

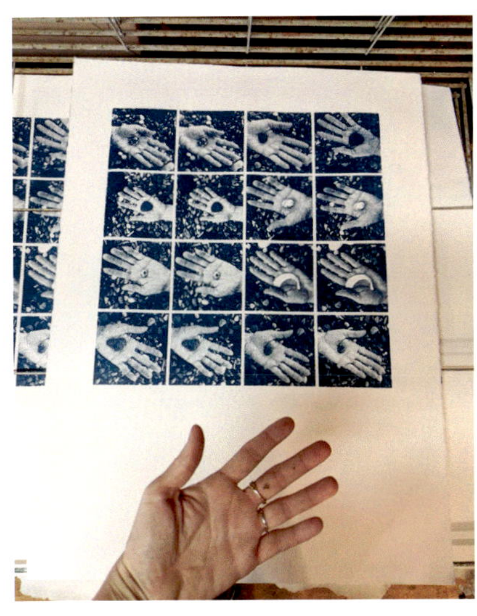

2.4
Instagram screenshot of
a recent print series by
Eve Biddle, featuring
pebbles and stones
collected from Guemes
Island, Washington, 2019.

2.5
Installation view of
Mary Ann Unger's *Wave*
(1989) in Tampa, Florida,
2008. Photo courtesy of
the Mary Ann Unger
Estate.

allow for contemporary values of thrift, sustainability, and care?

Eve I think if Mom could have cast everything in bronze, she would have. Anything! A few months ago, I learned that you can cast basalt now, and that set off all kinds of fires in my brain because we used to spend so much time up in Maine, and the coast of Maine has all these gorgeous basalt veins running through the granite. We would talk about all the geometry in nature while we were there and think about fractals and the Fibonacci sequence, and she would do all kinds of crazy things like lug a forty-pound rock from the ocean back to our loft in the city. To this day, I'm a real rock collector of pebbles and stones (fig. 2.4).

Anyway, I think there's real rigor and flexibility in her practice—and playfulness. There's a piece that got destroyed because it was made with concrete over an armature, and it just didn't survive outside. It was this big vertebra or a series of vertebrae that was very much like the *Across the Bering Strait* forms in that they arose out of the floor, but they were shorter, so it was like a spine along the ground. I remember the opening at the Trans Hudson Gallery: *Across the Bering Strait* was installed inside, and this concrete spine outside, and the kids were climbing all over it. And that was fine. The way the Louise Bourgeois sculptures live in the landscape at Williams College where you can get on it… It's amazing. That kind of playfulness… She took herself and her work very seriously, and yet there was this willingness to be playful. It wasn't like, "Oh, don't touch that now that it's made." It was like, "Oh, you won't damage it by touching it, go play hide-and-seek, have fun."

In terms of materials, it's really more a question of functionality and aesthetics. We want the work to have longevity in terms of its existence in the world, and it wants to be inter-acted with. Some of the public pieces, like the *Temple* (1986) and *Wave* (1989, fig. 2.5), in Tampa, are made out of

aluminum. And people touch them. You can hug them, squeeze your body into them, or walk into them or sit on them. In an ideal world, it doesn't matter what the material is as long as it maintains that responsive functionality. It's not kinetic. It's not moving. But it's interactive, and you can touch and feel it.

And there's a through line of aesthetics around color in her work, even the public work. It's something we saw as we started to install the estate retrospectively, ten or twelve years ago: the color palette across moments of her practice remains the same. There's this Pop Art-y, 1980s color, very New Mexico–inspired, in the public work; and there are the same colors later, just darker. All the colors that are in *Across the Bering Strait* are in all that Pop Art-y public work, they've just been darkened with additive pigment. But in terms of materials, it could be any-thing. The facilities and technologies available now to sculptors working at scale… some of them are cost prohibitive, but the possibili-ties are just amazing.

Sarah This is so interesting, because for some sculptors, bronze is a loaded material. To "tackle bronze" feels like going into history and has deep associations with statuary or permanence. And some find it a challenge they want to take on in order to conquer or unseat bronze. Others want to make their work as impermanent and as unbronze-like as possible. It seems like those questions were not your mother's concerns; it seems like, instead, bronze was one of many materi-als she was open to and was, perhaps, espe-cially excited to engage.

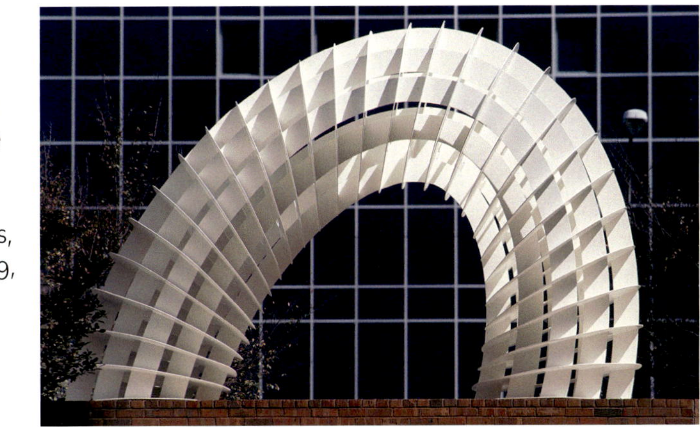

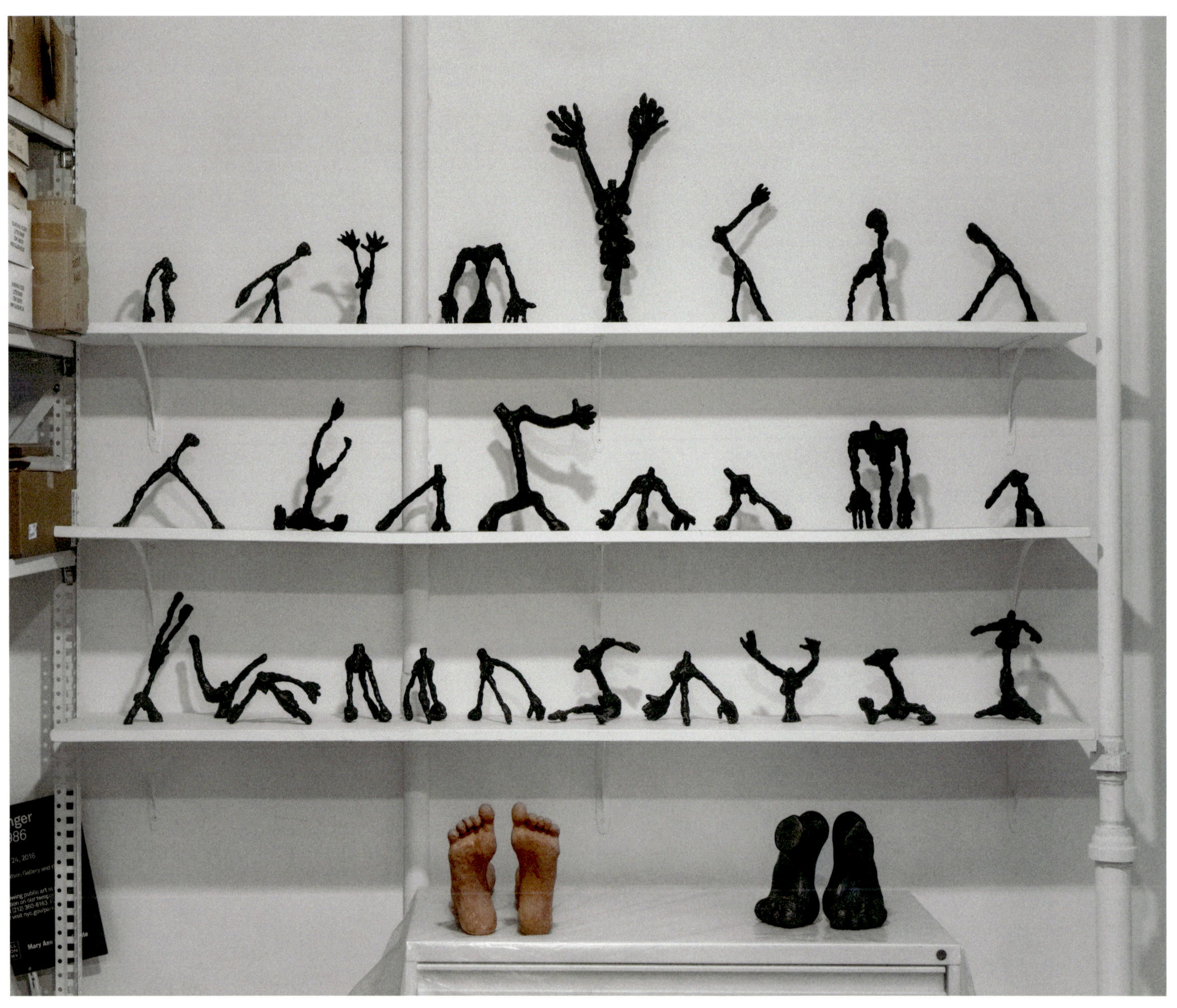

2.6
Installation view of a selection of the *Fragments*, Mary Ann Unger Estate, Third Street, New York, November 2021. Photo by Ryan Speth.

Ballard, Biddle, Montross

Eve Yes, absolutely. There are a number of bronze pieces that she did in her lifetime. The majority of the pieces were part of the series *Fragments*, which were small figurative sculptures, hand-sculpted in wax, over twigs and branches, and cast in bronze with lost-wax casting (fig. 2.6). They're not editioned. And there's one bronze piece that is a baby's head on a foot, and that's more formal in its sculpting and its finish; it's more Rodin-like in its rendering, but there's only one. Clearly, bronze was not the most interesting thing…

It's interesting to me to hear you talk about the gravitas of bronze as a material, because the things she produced in bronze are really, really playful. I remember her working on them in this little studio she rented in Maine. She'd go out to collect these sticks, and she worked that brown sculpting wax into workability because it was so hard. You can see all these finger marks in the bronze because of the force of her touch, and those fingerprints are somewhat related to what I'm working on in my own practice, but with a different motivation. And once you realize there's a stick armature under all that wax, you go, "Yup, there it is." It's very Giacometti inspired, but very casual, in a certain way.

Horace I was thinking along those same lines of the casual essence, but the intuition and the intention are always right there. We talk a lot about rigorous play, and the formalities and the function of play. Unger synthesizes those modalities in ways that are unique and generous for our own looking, conveying a sense in some works, like the *Fragments*, of the amorphous and sensual nature of both wax and molten bronze, their malleability and mutability, which throws into relief their hardness when at resting temperature. She's working at such a high caliber.

Might we add another dimension to the conversation? Mary Ann Unger was your mother, and was from a family of artists and engineers. You yourself are an artist, from a family of artists and engineers. You have a wonderfully rich practice as an artist, and you are one of the great galvanizers of artistic community, both in the region and in the country. I'm wondering, and this is a huge question, how your parents' respective practices influence your own sense of being an artist?

Eve That's a really big question. In a certain way, we can begin with the question, What is the definition of success in a life, or in an artistic practice? I think, for my parents (though Dad has had the time to grow beyond this in a really wonderful and profound way), thirty years ago, it was kind of MoMA or bust, and that was limited. Their practices and their activities weren't limited; they did public art and showed with galleries. But I remember reading through Mom's journals after her death and seeing notes like, "I'm fifty and still no gallery." You know, brutal. That was a big measure of success. She had very traditional measures of success. In the 1970s and '80s, there started to be viable alternatives to that model of mainstream success, but I think part of what I was thinking about in my twenties was setting goals I knew I could succeed at and figuring out what could I do.

I started making paintings and experimenting after college and realized it wasn't for me. My first growing out of that was when I started doing public murals, and those were collaborative with Josh Frankel, my husband, and community based, on the Groundswell model. We did our first murals through New York Cares, working with community and collaboratively with students to form ideas and put their ideas out in the world, and that was really invigorating for me. Bowie Zunino and I started collaborating together, making art first, and doing collaborative art happenings and events while she was still at RISD, back in 2008. Wassaic Project also began around August 2008. And that was great.

I was coming out of a season of reading about social practice and about Rick Lowe and Theaster Gates, and then meeting them, and looking at artists who were working in different directions. Rick is an interesting example of that because he has Project Row Houses, but he also has his own practice, and he's doing all these collaborations, and he's working with institutions, and then I started thinking about this more and realizing,

"Oh, I really can choose my own adventure here." In 2010, I started working alongside and thinking more with Mom's work, and then in 2012 or 2014, I was like, "Oh, these aren't separate at all. That's just totally make-believe. It's always all together, and people can engage with whatever they want, but it's all here, all right here."

There's this funny thing happening with the spectrum of work, with Wassaic Project on one end, with its international crop of artists and everything collaboratively minded and really social, and then my own ceramic practice is the opposite of collaborative. It's me in my studio, alone, with just my hands, at a scale that implies "only I am touching this thing." If we want to get metaphorical, both practices are about putting a piece of myself out there in the world, whether it is about getting people together or imbuing an object with a part of myself. Even the Unger Estate's recent initiative of curatorial fellows stems from this spectrum of work, of doing whatever it takes to make the best thing. That gathering of folk together and that generosity of spirit runs throughout, and that's true of working with my dad's photos now too.

Sarah I've been reading Horace's essay about Unger, and I learned about the way your family socialized and the modeling through your parents that could seed something like the Wassaic Project. It seems like the tools and the lessons from your childhood resonate in your life choices and practices, and that's really inspiring.

Eve I've been thinking about that too. There was a kind of radical acceptance in my household as a kid. Greer Lankton was my babysitter, Sylvia Netzer and Gloria Klein were Mom's friends. It was just, "Are you kind and interesting? Great. Come to dinner, let's hang out."

Horace I want to amplify that sense of gathering and what it means to be gathered into the galvanizing presence of Unger's work and be brought into conversation around it. During this year of pandemic and political change, Unger's life and art, and the inextri-

cable weave between them, has been a kind of constant companion throughout such dis-ease in the body politic and the world.

Eve It's interesting to think back to what was modeled in the context of the pandemic. Mom was sick for a long time. She was sick for fourteen years. And I don't really remember her complaining. Ever. There was never, "Why me, this sucks, I'm miserable." I'm sure Dad got more of it than I did, but there was none of it for me. And I took that for granted. You get dealt a rough deal, you've got to deal with it and make the best of it. Obviously, there are cultural contexts where that is not an appropriate or best response, but that was something that was modeled for personal behavior with my own life experiences. I'm not advocating or putting that forward as a model for acceptance of all hardship in any way, but there was a real resilience and an ability to take what you had and look on the bright side, so to speak, that I appreciate in my life.

But this sense, or lesson of modeling for me as an artist, also comes through in the sense of playfulness and material. Mary Ann was game for experimentation. Let's work in plaster, let's work in bronze, let's work in Hydrocal, let's work in steel armatures, okay, let's try this concrete on top, let's try bonded iron or this weird, experimental material. She did glass casting at one point, molds, painting, graphite, prints, gouache, watercolor, totally comfortable with all of the above. That's totally wild, and you get there by experimenting and taking life as it comes. And also, in a certain sense, being willing to fail. All things considered, it was a pretty short career to have covered all this ground. Oh yeah, she also did wood, these little balsawood models that are super detailed and painted sometimes in flat color, sometimes more painterly, wire mesh… She was playful and expansive.

Sarah To what degree did Unger think about place and site?

Eve She thought about it a lot. There are some bonded-iron pieces still up at the house upstate, and those are probably the most resolved, as she lived with the site, but a

Ballard, Biddle, Montross

major part of her practice—especially in the 1980s—was publicly sited work. And part of that was strategic and entrepreneurial about how to make a living from these commissions: "Oh, let me fabricate these works myself and design them so I can." There was intense thought around what you pulled out in your essay, Horace, about how work can enhance a place, make a place more than what it is already through a sculptural intervention, which is an exciting way to think about public sculpture. This idea that public work is not just an intervention but is a conversation that connects people and the work and the place. You can see that happening in social media images of *Wave* in Tampa. People love that piece! They hang out with it and interact with it and walk their dogs by it. The idea that you can enhance place by engaging people is a critical piece of her thinking, even in the works that no longer exist.

Sarah This is all so important. My work involves looking at our landscape at deCordova and seeing the permanent collection and asking, "What is the history of sculpture we're telling here, when we have primarily white male artists in the collection?" I think the time period Unger is working in is really interesting, throughout the 1970s, '80s, and '90s when sculpture is changing. The medium had this real definition through the 1950s and '60s—we can name those modernist moments!—and then it changes, and I think Unger and her time period deserve some real close curatorial looking and scholarly connecting.

I've also been thinking through the question, Who are the inheritors of Unger's practice? Not necessarily whom she directly influenced, but rather the ideas in her work, that lineage of thought… Who are the folk carrying that forward? I was thinking of someone like Nancy Graves, whose work in the 1970s and '80s dealt with natural history, particularly resonances with bone. I was thinking about Agnes Denes, and about someone like Susan Rothenberg and avenues of her practice that deserve closer attention, especially the passages in some of her drawings where body parts are starting to

hinge or touch—not her *Horses* series, but those totemic isolations of form…

Eve [Rothenberg's drawings] remind me so much of the drawings for *Shanks*. Dad tells the story about having a lamb shank bone in the kitchen from something we ate and cleaning it and walking it down to Mom in the studio and saying, "I think you'd be interested in this." And then from this resultant drawing of a shank bone, the idea of another work in another material emerges. Separate but related.

Sarah Bones and their contexts for sculpture continue to be interesting and generative.

Horace I like your diachronic approach, Sarah, to look to the present and future. In the biographical essay, I was really trying to give Unger a cohort of folk—her mentors and teachers and circle, her influences, and the generation of female artists working in sculpture she would have read about and whose shows she would have seen and, in more cases than not, probably knew or had met in some way: Eva Hesse, Louise Bourgeois, Lynda Benglis, Kay Sekimachi… But I'd also love, at some point, to think of Unger and her experimentation in the same vein as we might think through the sculptural works and drawings of a Lygia Clark or Lygia Pape and that generation of LatinX *concretismo* or artists who think about traces of assemblage and embodied performance to get at themes of migration, political change and upheaval, and gender identity, like Senga Nengudi, ektor garcia, Nicki Cherry, Bel Falleiros, Esteban Ramòn Pérez, and also the tensile, poetic forms of Cecilia Vicuña and Maren Hassinger…

Eve … whom Stephanie Sparling-Williams (one of our inaugural curatorial fellows at the estate) is about to publish an article on, thinking through the exchange and confluence of ideas between Mom and Hassinger. Maren visited with Mom upstate (fig. 2.7)!

Horace Yes! So glad you raised up Stephanie's great research here. The seven elements of Hassinger's *Walking* (1978) are in the collection at WCMA, and we could not be more delighted. To have Hassinger and Unger together, alongside works in the collection by Kiki Smith and Ursula von Rydingsvard, will be incredible.

Sarah I've also been thinking of someone like Nairy Baghramian, whose work often deals with hinges, armatures, the connections between the wall and the floor, things like what Mary Ann's work was doing well before our present moment. Or Kate Newby, who thinks inside and outside institutional spaces, thinking through spatial textures and multiple configurations of time and space. And then, perhaps, someone like Julia Haft-Candell, who alludes to connections between bodies that get distorted. The broad questions these artists (in relationship to Unger) stimulate is, What is the futurity of Mary Ann Unger, and how to bring her attentions forward into the present moment?

Eve I think maybe Jerry Saltz said something like, "They're dead. Who cares?!" I think he said this in the context of "Let's pay attention to living artists," and my brain is in that world. But you know, for my mom, it's just to have the conversation. Her generation didn't get their due attention until they were in their seventies, and now look at Kiki Smith and Ursula von Rydingsvard and these other female rock stars having these major, major shows when they're older. They lived longer than Mary Ann, and yes, their careers were a bit farther along at the moment she died too; but I just want her to be part of the conversation. That's ultimately, in my heart, what I really want. I just want there to be an acknowledgment of that influence and what is canonical and how can we expand that idea.

My little sister, who is fourteen, introduced me the other day to the idea of a "head canon." For example, in the world of *Harry Potter*, canon is what is written, and head canon is reading between the lines to get to a sense of what you want to be written;

basically, what is there and present but not explicitly determined or stated in the text. And every artist has a head canon of sorts, artists they're thinking about or artists they're looking at, whether they're conscious of it or not. I would say every artist has conscious and unconscious influences, and I would love for Mary Ann's work to percolate into the consciousness for more artists. Given her training and her connections throughout the art world while she was alive, and given the exposure she has had since her death, her work is out there and present, and I think the work is pretty unusual if not unique for that era, and maybe still is to this day. And I think that is worth being in our consciousness.

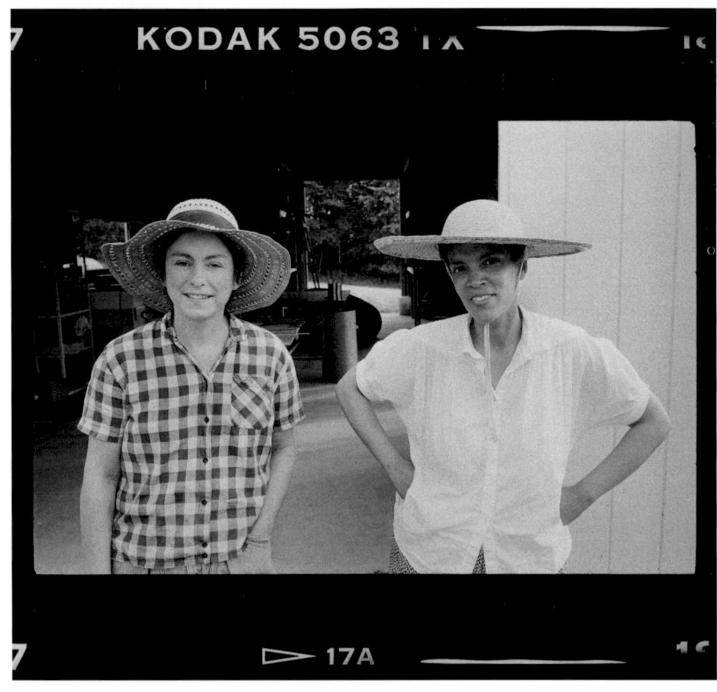

2.7
Mary Ann Unger and Maren Hassinger, Wallkill, New York, 1990. Photo by Geoffrey Biddle. Courtesy of the artist.

Ballard, Biddle, Montross

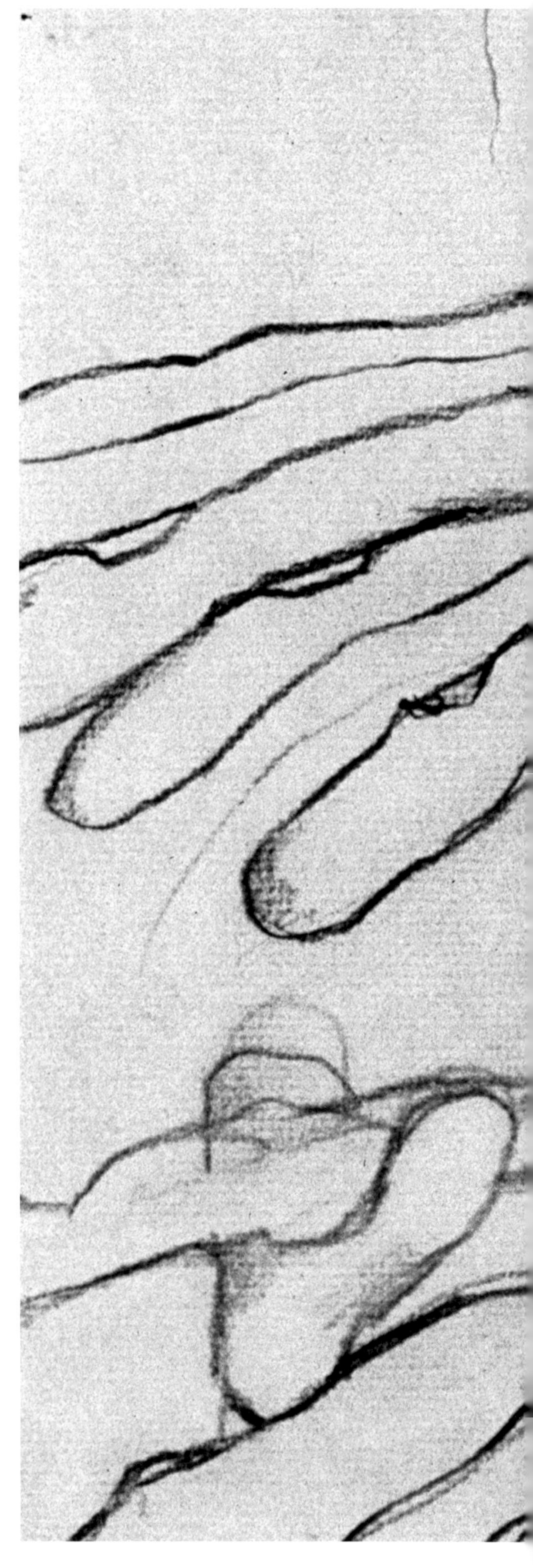

Mary Ann Unger, *Study for Across the Bering Strait*, 1992, graphite on paper, 22¼ × 30 in. ID 1080. Collection of the Mary Ann Unger Estate. Image courtesy of the Mary Ann Unger Estate.

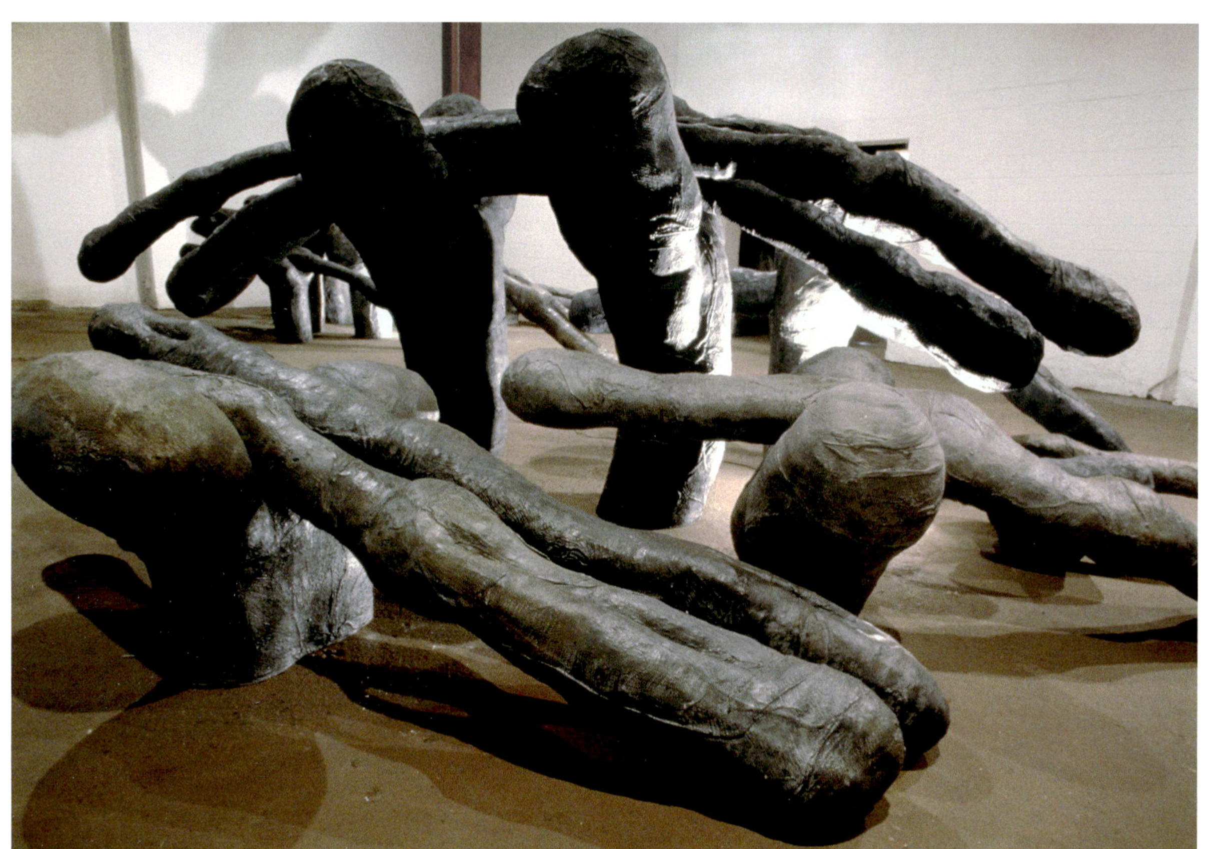

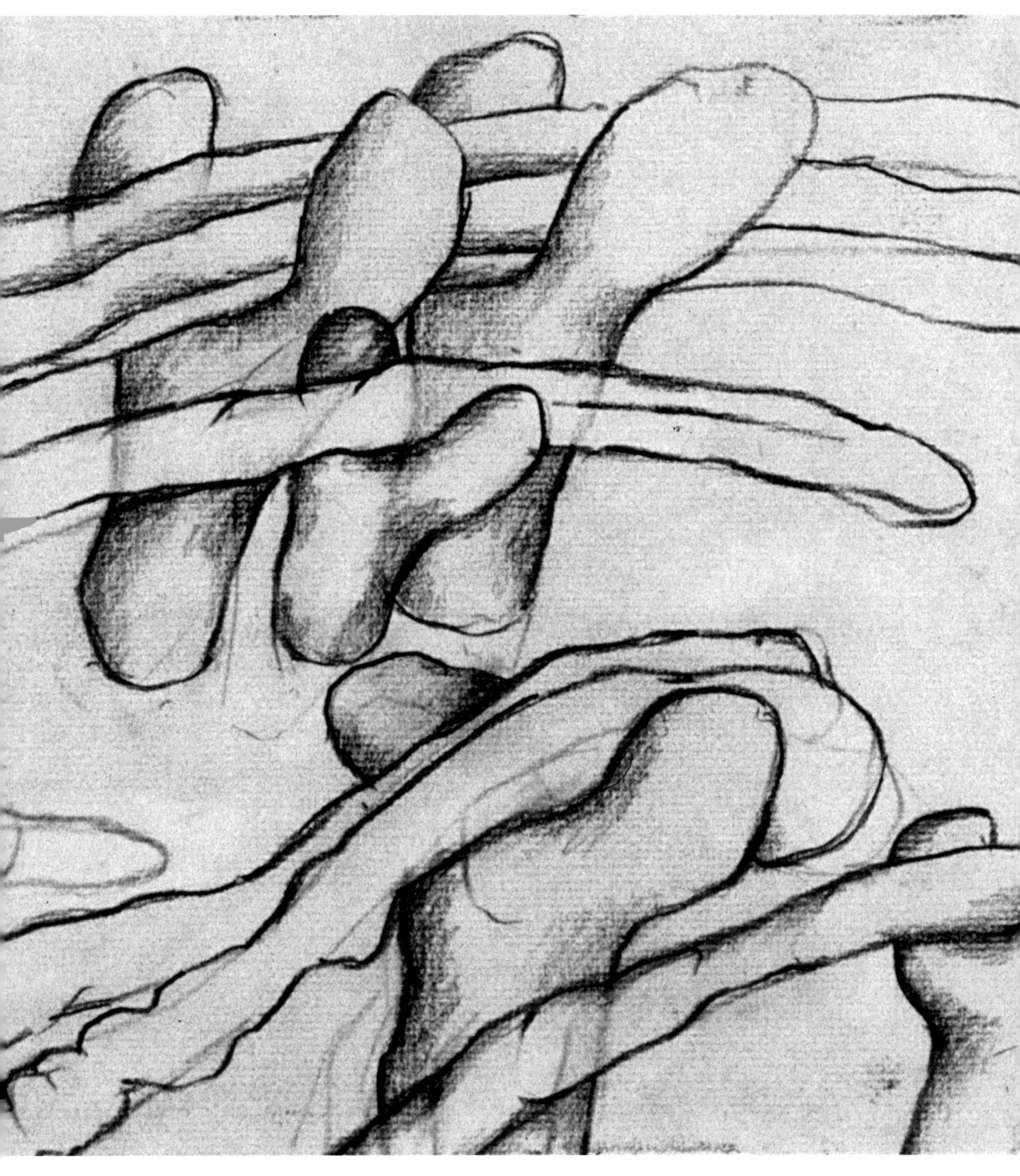

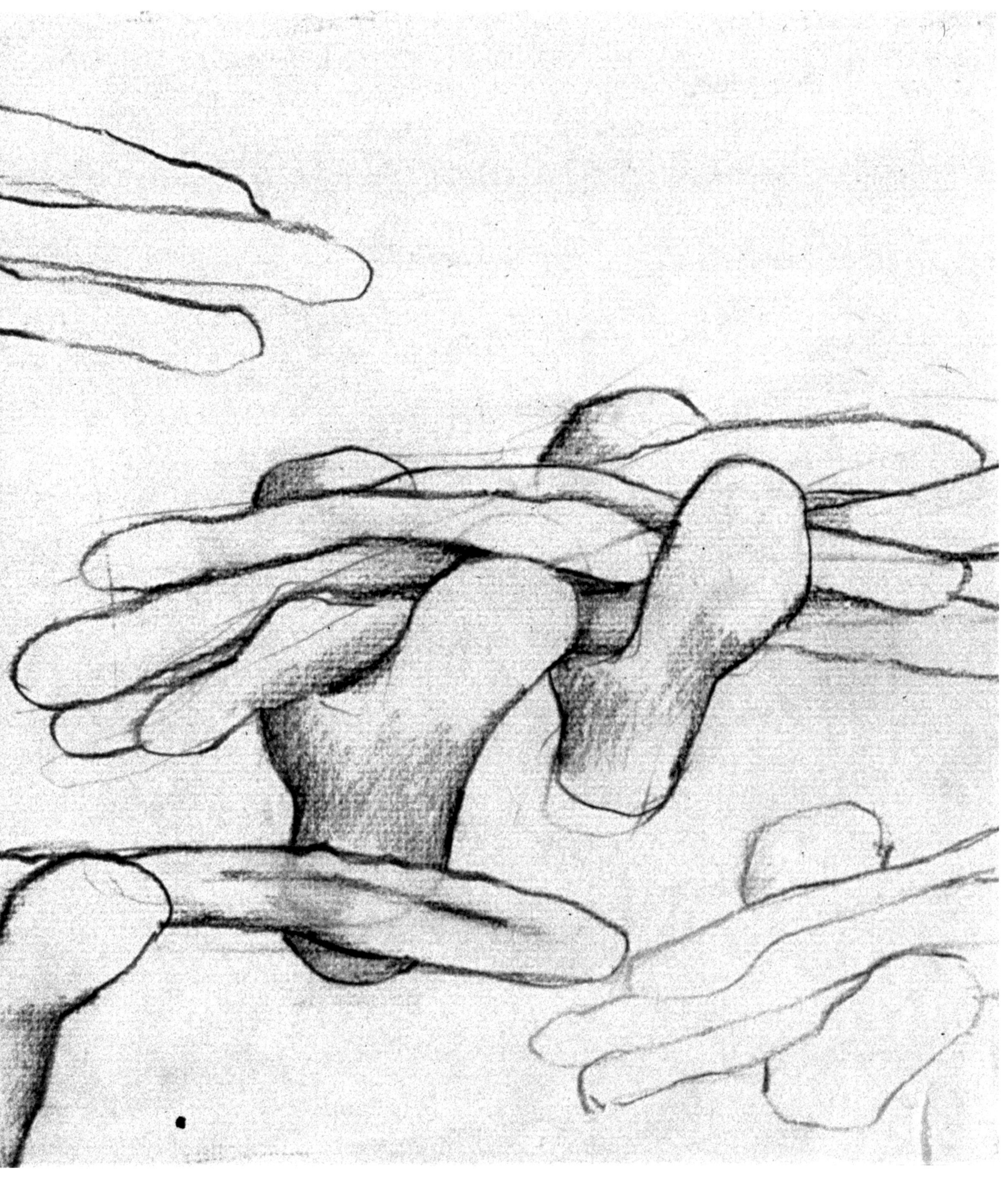

The Things We Carry

Mary Ann Unger's *Across the Bering Strait*

Zoe Dobuler

3.1
Mary Ann Unger, *Across the Bering Strait*, 1992–94 (detail), Hydrocal over steel with pigment and graphite, 55 × 33 × 6 ft. Collection of the Mary Ann Unger Estate. Image courtesy of the Mary Ann Unger Estate.

Snaking across the gallery, the three dozen constituent parts of Mary Ann Unger's *Across the Bering Strait* (1992–94) hold, cradle, lean on, support, and carry one another (figs. 3.1–3.4). In abstracted post-and-lintel-like groupings, the horizontal and vertical elements, which stretch between ten and fourteen feet long, are fluid and organic, with rounded protuberances creating a gently undulating surface. Visually, the individual pieces recall the gnarled fingers of an outstretched hand, the irregular forms of tree branches, or microscopic life-forms enlarged to a superhuman scale. Or perhaps they are the bones of giants, bundles of nerves, or even a funeral procession. Although the parts are abstract, they have, according to the artist, a "distinctly figurative aspect" that generates narrative and allows for bodily identification with the work, as if another body were sharing the gallery space.[1] But just what those identifications are is left purposefully undefined.

When viewed as an ensemble, the work evokes broader, more metaphorical resonances, and the interpretive possibilities proliferate. The vertical "posts" and horizontal "lintels" they support conjure infrastructure such as bridges or ramps, which necessarily bring to mind those who may be traveling across them; the Y-shaped posts become outstretched arms carrying possessions or perhaps other bodies across the gallery. A closer look at the sculpture's textured surface reveals visible wrapping and bandaging, raising questions of whether the bodies alluded to are alive or dead, wounded or perhaps mummified. A focus on the surface also draws the viewer's attention to the simple but easily overlooked fact of the sculpture's potential interior space—what does the work carry inside?

Describing the piece in an artist statement, Unger initially characterized *Across the Bering Strait* as an "abstract sculpture about migration."[2] Although the size and configuration of elements may change with each installation, the themes of walking, carrying, and striving toward a goal are constant; the work's abstraction and embodied sensibility allow it to slide across physical, temporal, and cosmic scales, from the infinitesimal to the gigantic, the prehistoric to the contemporary, the personal to the universal. The installation's title explicitly refers to a theory about early humans' migration into North America that was prominent through the 1990s, which posited that migrants first crossed from Asia into present-day Alaska over a land bridge that connected the two continents during the Pleistocene era.[3] According to the theory, humanity then spread eastward and southward, giving rise to populations that are the distant ancestors of today's Native American, First Nations,

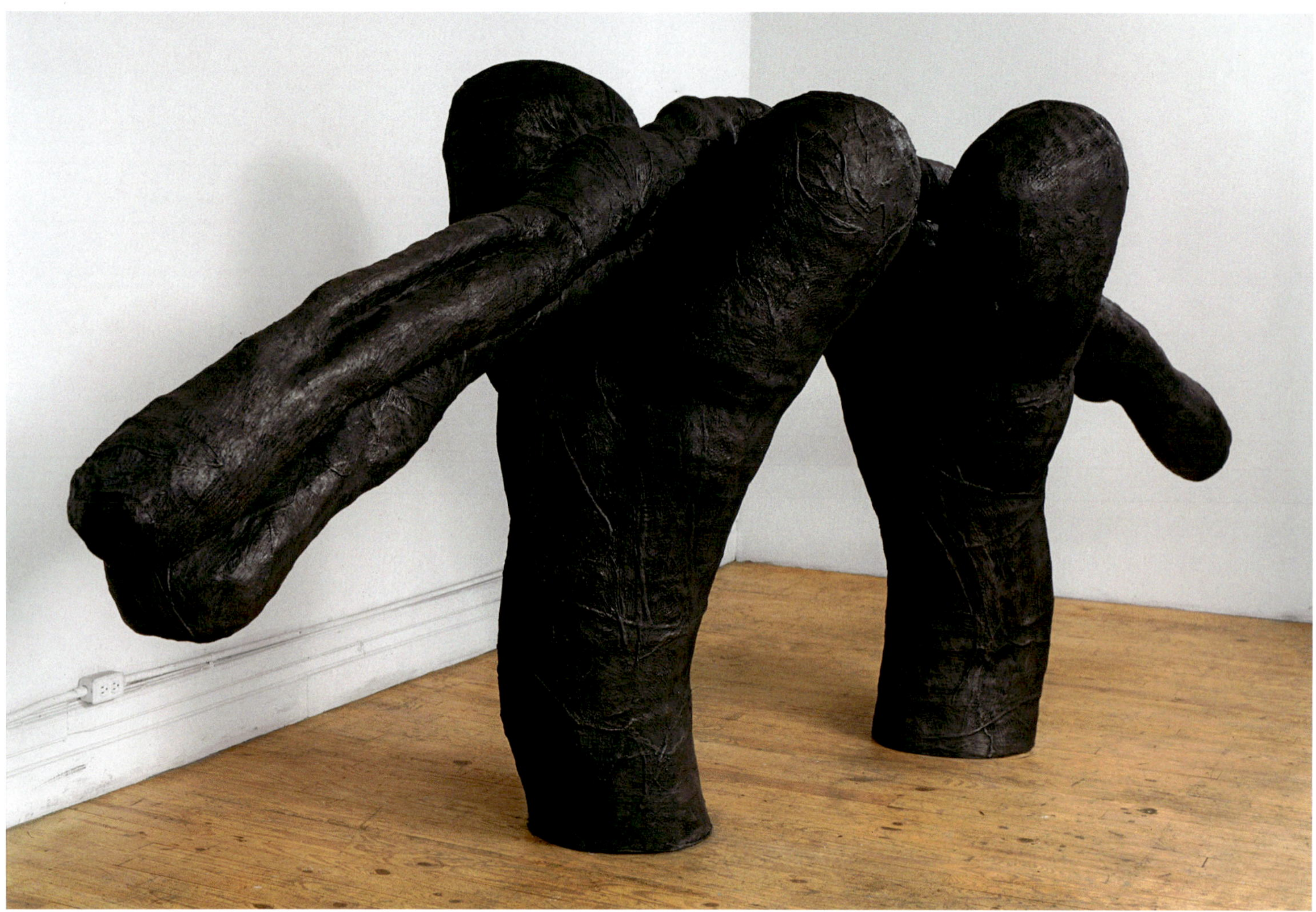

3.2
Mary Ann Unger, *Across the Bering Strait*, 1992–94 (detail), Hydrocal over steel with pigment and graphite, 55 × 33 × 6 ft. Collection of the Mary Ann Unger Estate. Image courtesy of the Mary Ann Unger Estate.

and other Indigenous communities in North and South America.

Though the work's title references a specific historical phenomenon, Unger notes that the resonances of that ancient migration extend through time into the present, joining the prehistoric experience of early humans with the individual experiences of more contemporary immigrants: the work "evokes memories of our primeval history and suggests a continuity between the journeys of our ancestors and our journeys today."[4] Unger further connects this theme to her own personal mythology; she describes her family history within the Jewish diaspora and her relatives' immigration to the United States as a reenactment of what she calls the ongoing, millennia-long "saga of the wandering Jew."[5] Through these shifts in scale,

Across the Bering Strait is able to represent and connect, simultaneously, a broad historical phenomenon and a distinctly individual experience, like a myth wavering between the realms of the symbolic and the intimately personal. The sculpture's form also communicates this duality. Interpreted as the means of travel—as a collection of bridges or ramps—it can call to mind the expansive tale of human movement; Unger, however, suggested that the posts are "torsolike" and the lintels "limblike," generating an alternate understanding that casts the work as a representation of individual migrants with bodies that could be our ancestors', or our own.[6]

Unger also notes that these migrants are not traveling empty-handed. As they roam, traversing borders or continents or epochs,

Dobuler

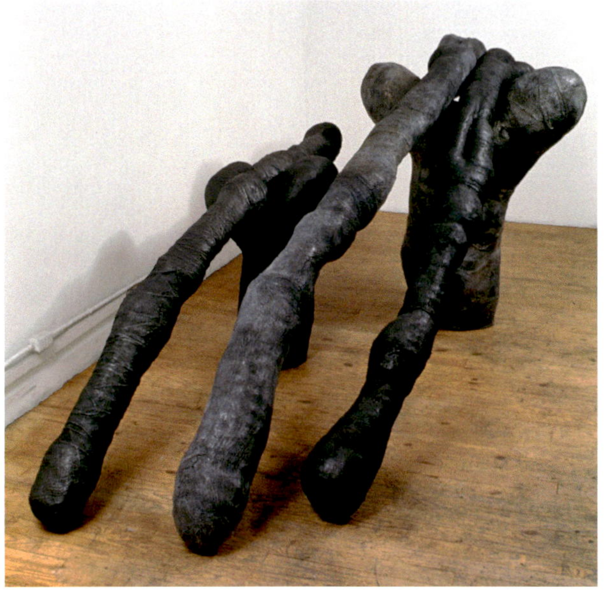

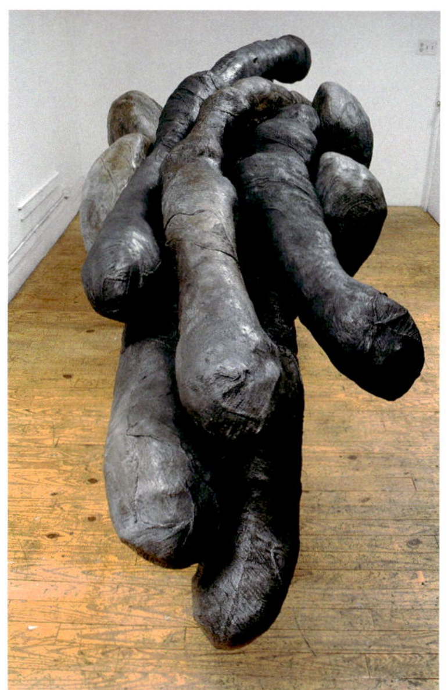

3.3
Mary Ann Unger, *Across the Bering Strait* (detail), 1992–94, Hydrocal over steel with pigment and graphite, 55 × 33 × 6 ft. Collection of the Mary Ann Unger Estate. Image courtesy of the Mary Ann Unger Estate.

3.4
Mary Ann Unger, *Across the Bering Strait* (detail), 1992–94, Hydrocal over steel with pigment and graphite, 55 × 33 × 6 ft. Collection of the Mary Ann Unger Estate. Image courtesy of the Mary Ann Unger Estate.

"they carry their nationalities and cultures with them," she writes, "just as they carry their possessions."[7] That both one's physical belongings and more immaterial qualities can be carried either by or within a human body points to an expansive interpretation of the verb and its potential direct and indirect objects. We may carry items and goods, but also information and knowledge. We are carriers of disease, genetic traits, and ancestry. We carry names, burdens, traumas, and traditions. We can also carry bodies, either our own as we move through the world or those of our children or our dead. This perennial carrying has significant implications for making meaning not only of *Across the Bering Strait* but also of human experience. Unger's statement continues:

> We may have our hopes for an information superhighway and our dreams of an interconnected world in the technological twenty-first century, yet it [is] still the movements of peoples that make us aware of each other around the world: migration is arguably the strongest force towards the creation of a global village. Just as it made the world larger thirty thousand years ago, it is still people moving, migrating, and even literally walking, that is making the world smaller today.[8]

Instead of digital technologies, it is people—an analog "information superhighway" of embodied beings full of biological, intellectual, and cultural information—moving throughout the world who serve as the primary mechanisms of transmission. Individuals' capacity to carry is thus their most important contribution to the formation of a greater humanity.

According to author Ursula K. Le Guin, the metaphor of carrying is also effective when applied to storytelling and conveying meaning through narrative. In her influential 1986 essay "The Carrier Bag Theory of Fiction," which was republished in 2019, Le Guin argues that the novel's highest form is that of the carrier or container, something that can hold the myriad, even conflicting, ideas and interpretations that characterize lived existence.[9] The title of her essay might be familiar to some, as it references "The Carrier Bag Theory of Evolution," a chapter from Elizabeth Fisher's 1979 book *Woman's Creation: Sexual Evolution and the Shaping of Society*, which reexamined prevailing theories of human development through a feminist lens. Among Fisher's most prominent claims was a challenge to the idea, popular among her contemporaries, that hunting was "the master behavior pattern" leading to the ascendance of man.[10] Instead, she submits the "invention of the carrier bag as the take-off point" for the development of humanity.[11] In Fisher's estimation, the first and most consequential "cultural device" was not a weapon but rather "a recipient"; humanity's innovation—what allowed us to become "human" as we know ourselves to be today—was the humble act of carrying, not a grand feat of violence.[12] Fisher supports this assertion with archaeological and biological evidence suggesting that many of the earliest people, living millions of years ago, subsisted primarily on vegetation accumulated through gathering, rather than on meat garnered through hunting.[13] Incidentally, since women were often responsible for food gathering and for transporting infants, Fisher posits that they were likely the originators of the carrier bag, which would have been essential for the storage of food and would have, in turn, allowed early peoples to develop more sophisticated behaviors and societal structures.

In her essay, Le Guin finds a relationship between Fisher's account of the origins of humanity and the creation of fiction; what the carrier bag was to the early humans, the novel is to Le Guin's contemporary moment. In the symbolism of the carrier bag, Le Guin locates an alternate mode of storytelling, one that challenges the dominance of the singular heroic narrative and calls attention to the other voices that the hero's presence silences. The (typically male) hero's journey, facilitated by a weapon, forces outward, away, while the novel, like the carrier bag, "brings energy home."[14] As she explains, "I would go so far as to say that the natural, proper, fitting shape of the novel might be that of a sack, a bag. A book holds words. Words hold things. They bear meanings. A novel is a medicine bundle, holding things in a particular, powerful relation to one another and to us."[15] Meaning is therefore conceptualized as a multitude, an ecology that, in its shift away from a teleology represented by the weapon-wielding protagonist, opens the door to a sense of ongoingness. It encourages the acceptance of complex, even unresolved narratives that can more accurately reflect the realities and vagaries of lived experience.

Unger's description of *Across the Bering Strait* at a 1994 gallery talk positions the work as perhaps the logical extension of these two Carrier Bag Theories—Fisher's of evolution and Le Guin's of fiction. Unger began by framing her discussion of the sculpture in terms of the "language of the holder and the held" that she had been developing in the 1990s.[16] After mentioning the open-endedness of the work ("it's about migration or a journey, or about carrying the dead home from war, or whatever"), she goes on to remark, "The point is that it has a lot of references, which is what I want from my work. The more you can find in it, obviously the richer it is. And I think… this gives you a greater freedom to bring your thoughts to the piece, and also it gives my work a greater resonance with you if it has more stories in it for you."[17] In addition to adopting carrying as its primary visual allusion, *Across the Bering Strait* also adopts its metaphysics. Unger stresses the relevance of multiple interpretations and the importance of viewers' varying perspectives in establishing the meaning of the work. She gives us license to integrate the piece into our lives, and vice versa. Unger's generous permission likens her work to Le Guin's novel, a recipient that holds the profusion of stories that make us human, as diverse as they may be.

This interpretation accepts, even encourages, contradiction, advocating for a more collaborative, communal—and as Fisher and Le Guin would argue—feminine mode of world building. Fisher ties the carrier bag directly to the female form, pointing out that women were themselves "containers for children";[18] Le Guin contends that the novel-as-carrier-bag allows women—excluded when humanity's narrative is defined by masculine aggression—to feel fully represented, fully human, for the first time. Unger's practice is likewise heavily influenced by the female form, and she has commented that her more abstract pieces, including *Across the Bering Strait*, stem from her work with the figure that began in 1985 with sculptures like *Supplicant* (see fig. 1.16). That critical year also marked Unger's initial breast cancer diagnosis, beginning a battle that would last

Dobuler

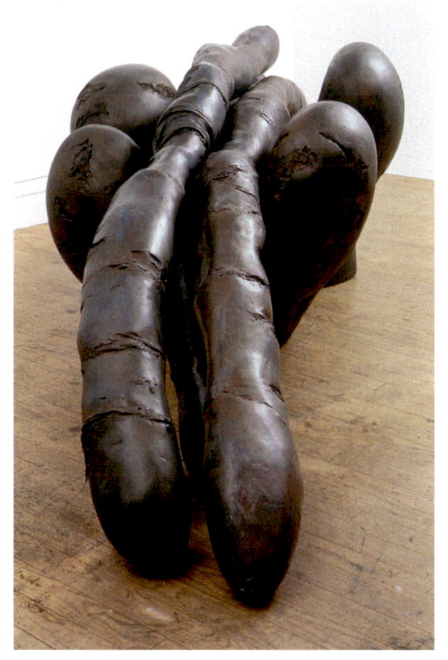

until her untimely death from the disease in 1998. *Supplicant* transforms her suffering—rooted in her physical body and in her breasts in particular—into a sort of totem or mythic embodiment. Four breast-like forms protrude from the sculpture's front surface, stacked one above the other. The anguished face of the work's head is craned upward, screaming in agony. With bulging eyes, the open mouth seems to emit a wail toward the sky. But its pain is transformative: referencing the ancient story of Apollo and Daphne, the figure's two arms metamorphose into a branch and leaf, respectively, before the viewer's eyes. As Unger wrote in a statement for *In a Dark Vein*, a 1989 exhibition she curated at New York's Sculpture Center, there is meaning to be found in "the paradox of wounds that heal and of pain that expresses an affirmation of life."[19]

Supplicant evinces another duality in Unger's works that can be traced through to *Across the Bering Strait*: the dialectic of trauma and healing, decay and regeneration, which appear at first opposed, but in reality necessitate one another. In *Across the Bering Strait*, the surface appears bandaged, as if the work has gravely damaged skin. The extent of the wrapping suggests the severity of the injury—but also the magnitude of the care administered. As critic Robert Taplin wrote, referring to Unger's 1991 sculpture

Deposition / Nature Mourned (fig. 3.5), the artist's use of bandaging "can also be read as swaddling," suggesting that her "forms [are] swollen with life rather than disease."[20] Both readings foreground the physicality of Unger's works and the strong, perhaps conflicting, bodily identifications that audiences experience when viewing them. Unger's Hydrocal sculptural process, which she developed over the late 1980s and early 1990s, contributes to this sensibility, as it "mirror[s] bodily construction and composition."[21] She first would construct a grid-like welded-steel armature—akin to a skeleton—which she would coat with a skin of cheesecloth soaked in Hydrocal plaster. Notably, Unger's method was completely additive; her hallmark "scarred" exteriors were created by building up the sides of each incision, rather than gouging or scraping away at the surface. Though it may present as the result of violent action or wear over time, the surface of *Across the Bering Strait* is actually the product of a "loving process" of infusion by Unger's hands.[22] As Sandy Harthorn has noted, Unger's process also generated a collapse between visual allusion and physical necessity: beyond the Hydrocal's ability to imitate skin, "Elements relating to branches and arms become metaphors for 'carrying life forces' in addition to being functional armatures for the sculpture. Likewise, bones and skeletal associations are more than figurative description, they refer to the physical support of the sculpture."[23] The associations Harthorn outlines hint at Unger's integration of Minimalism and post-Minimalism, evoking bodily organicism through a language of strict geometry. They also break down the boundaries between the sculpture's "body" and a human body, as the two come to occupy the same ontological space with relation to the broader world.

Therefore, the human body that *Across the Bering Strait* analogizes could be Unger's own, ravaged over the years by a debilitating cancer, but emerging, alive, on the other side. Unger's allusions to—and personal experiences with—corporeal suffering and illness have led many critics to find in her work a certain heroism, a stoic fortitude in the face of death and existential pain that has granted access to a kind of transcendent wisdom. And *Across the Bering Strait* could certainly be considered "heroic" in scale, its larger-than-life presence commanding the gallery space and reorienting viewers' movements around its sprawling limbs. But with Fisher's and Le Guin's ideas still fresh in our minds, how can we reconcile this seeming contradiction? For we know there is no room for the hero in the carrier bag. Yet it feels erroneous to strip the work of any piece of its affective power, to deny Unger credit for her courage and resilience, or to ask her, as did one *New York Magazine* critic, "to lighten up."[24] And rather than reduce its strength, the fleshlike quality of *Across the Bering Strait*'s bandaged surface and the resoluteness of its extension toward *something* engender a sense of heroism that is distinctly human, not super-human. Unger is able to balance the intimate and the prodigious, the intimidating and the vulnerable, to fashion a new, generous hero who is as much a victim of the world as its conqueror. It is almost an ordinary heroism, one that might befall someone unknowingly, or as they go about seemingly quotidian tasks—like, say, carrying something—that take on a larger significance.

    Across the Bering Strait inhabits a variable interpretive scale that moves smoothly along spectra of time, distance, and magnitude. It holds, like a bag, the stories of carriers both prehistoric and contemporary, well known and unnamed, heroic and ordinary. As Le Guin explains, the bag is also, and crucially, an equalizer: "You put [the hero] in the bag and he looks like a rabbit, a potato."[25] Instead of heroes, Le Guin's stories "have people in them"—but these people do extraordinary things.[26] In drawing out parallels and recurrences among seemingly disparate experiences and events, *Across the Bering Strait* performs a similar leveling. With this perspective, any task—from gathering food in a bag or walking slowly east across the Bering Land Bridge to battling an illness or making a sculpture—can slide from the everyday to the exceptional, the individual to the shared, the solitary to the latest in a long line that's come before. Little did the first migrants to North America Unger envisioned know that they represented the origins of the human species on the continent; they were, in all likelihood, looking for their next meal. The originator of the carrier bag was undoubtedly ignorant that her invention would, according to Fisher, precipitate major developments in her species' way of life. But with the benefit of perspective, Unger, like us, can see that these small acts have taken on outsized—one might even say heroic—significance. *Across the Bering Strait*, like the carrier bag, can hold these seeming contradictions, which in reality allow us to connect across history and geography.

Notes

Although not an explicit reference to Tim O'Brien's 1990 collection of short stories *The Things They Carried*, the title of this essay was in part inspired by it and by the powerful evocations his book has lent to the phrase.

1. Mary Ann Unger, Artist's Statement [third-person], "Across the Bering Strait," c. 1992–95, Mary Ann Unger Estate. Unger wrote two almost identical, undated artist's statements for *Across the Bering Strait*, both reproduced in this volume on pp. 86–87. The primary difference is in point of view: they include a first-person and a third-person treatment. For the purposes of clarity across the volume, the statements will be distinguished as such.

2. Unger, Artist's Statement [third-person].

3. During Unger's lifetime, the Bering Strait Land Bridge theory of migration into North America was favored among the scientific community, with one scholar writing in 1989 that archaeologists were "practically unanimous" in their support for this hypothesis. More recently, however, new archaeological and geological findings that posit alternative origins for the early population of the continent have challenged the land-bridge theory. It is also important to note that many Indigenous communities have consistently rejected the land-bridge hypothesis for humanity's origins in North and South America.

4. Unger, Artist's Statement [third-person].

5. Mary Ann Unger, Artist's Statement [first-person], "Across the Bering Strait," c. 1992–95, Mary Ann Unger Estate.

6. Unger, Artist's Statement [third-person].

7. Unger, Artist's Statement [third-person].

8. Unger, Artist's Statement [third-person].

9. Ursula K. Le Guin, *The Carrier Bag Theory of Fiction* (New York: Ignota, 2019).

10. Elizabeth Fisher, *Woman's Creation: Sexual Evolution and the Shaping of Society* (New York: McGraw-Hill, 1979), 56.

11. Fisher, *Woman's Creation*, 56.

12. Fisher, *Woman's Creation*, 58.

13. Interestingly, Fisher notes one exception when presenting evidence for her theory that many prehistoric populations survived predominantly on gathered food: Arctic peoples (living sixty degrees or more from the equator), such as those crossing the Bering Strait Land Bridge. Above a certain latitude, hunting likely replaced gathering as the foremost source of food, as flora cannot easily survive in such harsh environments. This may, at first, appear contradictory to the arguments presented here. However, Fisher is writing about early peoples living millions of years ago who, she posits, invented the carrier bag; the populations that may have crossed the Bering Strait Land Bridge did so as recently as tens of thousands of years ago. Second, as it was for Le Guin, Fisher's theories' relevance to storytelling and the creation of fiction is paramount to scientific specificity.

14. Le Guin, *Carrier Bag Theory of Fiction*, 30.

15. Le Guin, *Carrier Bag Theory of Fiction*, 34.

16. Mary Ann Unger, in "Abstraction as a Timeless Art Form," Artists Talk on Art, panel moderated by Clement Meadmore, with John L. Moore, Robert Murray, Peter Stroud, Martin Bull, and Mary Ann Unger, Fulcrum Gallery, SoHo, New York, January 21, 1994. Artists Talk on Art Records, circa 1974–2018, Archives of American Art, Smithsonian Institution.

17. Unger, in "Abstraction as a Timeless Art Form."

18. Fisher, *Woman's Creation*, 60.

19. Mary Ann Unger, *In a Dark Vein* (New York: Sculpture Center, 1989).

20. Robert Taplin, "Mary Ann Unger at Klarfeld Perry," *Art in America*, June 1992, 106.

21. Sandy Harthorn, *Fabricated Nature* (Boise, ID: Boise Art Museum, 1994), 42.

22. Eve Biddle in conversation with the author, July 16, 2020.

23. Harthorn, *Fabricated Nature*, 10.

24. Kay Larson, "Small Wonders," *New York Magazine*, March 30, 1992.

25. Le Guin, *Carrier Bag Theory of Fiction*, 35.

26. Le Guin, *Carrier Bag Theory of Fiction*, 35.

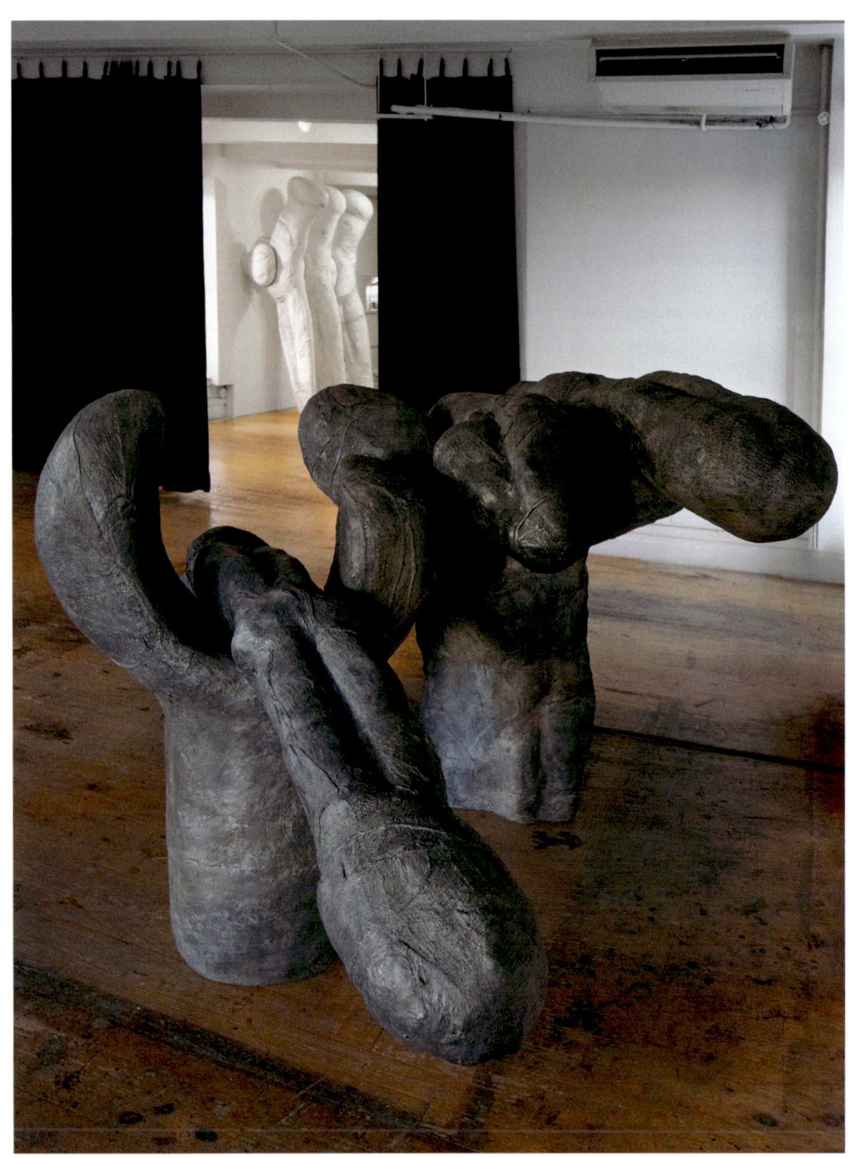

Power Objects
Forms to Rival the Moon

Horace D. Ballard

I first learned of Mary Ann Unger's practice in 2018. I had met Unger's daughter, Eve Biddle, at a cocktail party in New York two months before.[1] I was curious about Eve's practice as an artist and her work with the Wassaic Project, which she cofounded and codirects. I was greatly interested in the work of her father, photographer Geoffrey Biddle, as well. Eve invited me down to the city for a visit to the Mary Ann Unger Estate, and I readily accepted.

On that temperate Friday morning in early March, we walked up to the eighth floor of the building on Third Street, and Eve Biddle opened the door. Unger's sculpture *Shanks* (1996–97, see fig. 1.25) greeted us. It was installed against the wall between two windows facing the door as sunlight poured through. The work pulsed with such power and self-regard: its tensile forms soaking up the light and refracting it around the space, becoming, for a moment, extensive and vitreous. I must have audibly gasped, because Biddle said, "If you like that, you should see…"

Biddle walked across my vision and disappeared behind a pair of blackout curtains. She pushed them apart to reveal another third of the loft and its "residents." And that was how I encountered the multiple elements of Unger's monumental *Across the Bering Strait* (1992–94, fig. 4.1; see figs. 3.1–3.4). I was mesmerized. I think I said

something grand, like "Wow." I think I probably tried to follow it up with something more "curatorial," like "The forms are so powerful and yet not insistent, even as they completely reshape the architecture of the space." I definitely remember saying, "Oh my god, Eve, what am I even seeing right now?!"

That is when Biddle told me about her mother's work and the mission of the estate. She promised to put me in touch with the estate's director, Allison Kaufman, and the Davidson Gallery, which represents the estate. We spent more than an hour walking around and through *Across the Bering Strait* before turning to other works by Unger, installed throughout the space. What was meant to be a midmorning chat turned into a full day's immersion. I was enchanted by the formal particularities of the work and by Biddle's and the estate's fearlessness in interrogating the big questions of a practice. We riffed and reflected across dozens of works in various media about various critical angles of the practice that an academic museum could take on—offering various generative contexts for students learning about contemporary curatorial practice and scholarly research.

In that first encounter, it was Biddle who initiated a conversation about how the original sound component for the monumental work was appropriated from Inuit chants,

4.1
Installation view of an element of Mary Ann Unger's *Across the Bering Strait* (1992–94), looking toward a glimpse of *Shanks* (1996–97) in the background, Mary Ann Unger Estate, November 2021. Photo by Horace Ballard.

"

and how *Across the Bering Strait* came out of Unger's independent research into her family's migration to the United States, and also into ancient/Indigenous migration to the Americas. But even with the purest intentions, employing the aural and visible traces of cultures and histories not indelibly linked to our personal stories is sticky. Biddle was hopeful that the next fulsome presentation of her mother's work would tackle the stickiness of appropriation/appreciation head-on.[2]

I left galvanized by the openness of Unger's family, the Davidson Gallery, and the estate. I left knowing I wanted to make an exhibition and write about the work. As I rode the train back along the Hudson River at sunset, I started sketching and formulating words around what I had seen. The journey from those early ideas to the exhibition would take four years. And the world has changed even more. But the power of Unger's process and language remain.

It is now mid-February of 2021, and it is snowing. From my window, if I chose to look, I could see a mountain rising through the ubiquitous February veil of falling sky over the southern Vermont hills.

But I am not attending to the world as it is/being made anew; I am riveted to a moment nearly thirty years ago. On the computer screen, the SMPTE color bars tremolo to white snow. A grainy moving image appears, and as a human figure walks into the frame, the image relaxes into focus. The body is so proximate to the camera's lens at first that the figure is obscured in digital shade, except for the occasional flash of teeth and the upper half of a Fair Isle wool sweater that swings occasionally into and then out of the anterior light.

This is Mary Ann Unger, on a January night in 1994, giving an artist's talk at the Fulcrum Gallery, SoHo. The voice is striking. The hair is short, spiky, matter-of-fact. The right arm gestures in arching port de bras, extending and deepening the planar scene. The fingers of that hand curl and point, kneading the air around it as they indicate specific passages in the slide image, noting that while the audience takes the indexed flatness of the object as fact, the artist speaking knows, shaped, formed this work in three dimensions. I am riveted. Let's listen in:

The abstraction I'm working with right now comes out of my working with the figure, beginning in 1985. *Next slide, please.* This, this comes out of an encounter with a very serious illness. It's pretty obvious that it was breast cancer. This piece, these pieces I'm showing you, their power, come out of moments when I am fully in the emotion of it, which is not really what abstraction is about, but I want you to notice some of the elements in this piece because it enriched the work that would come in the future. *Next slide, please.* There's the idea of mythology: Daphne, the woman who becomes a tree, you can see both arms are "becoming": one is a twig, one is a leaf. *Next slide, please.* There's a reference to the *Guernica* cry/scream [Picasso, 1937] and that becomes an element in some of my future works, and then this multiple-breast image, something I use quite a bit, sourced from older references.[3]

Though unnamed in the talk, the work of which Unger speaks, is *Supplicant* (1985, see fig. 1.16). In a review of an exhibition Unger curated years earlier, Michael Brenson, sculpture critic for the *New York Times*, wrote of *Supplicant*:

> Modeled in Hydrocal and then carved, it presents a large bald head almost impaled on a spine supporting four vertically aligned breasts. The figure has small, outstretched arms that suggest leaves or the wings of a prehistoric bird. The mouth is huge and wide open to the sky. The breasts project forward, like offerings or gun barrels. If the outstretched wings suggest a frantic desire for flight, they also make the figure, with her open mouth, seem operatic. The work is both a cry of pain and a song of faith.[4]

As I have since learned, the power of Mary Ann Unger's practice arises from the possibilities and constraints of the personal. Her intelligence is neither narrow, linear, nor

Ballard

defined by discipline. Unger's practice is animated by the ways in which cultural myth, disease, and the structural impositions on women and women's bodies traverse society and self in a cycle of excavation that continually raises the depths of the psyche to the surface of skin. And somewhere in this moment of the artist's talk, in the winter of 1994, is the key to understanding the work of the last fifteen years of her life.

"It's pretty obvious," Unger tells the assembled listeners, "that I felt that I had been through an experience drawing me into darkness, and now perhaps I was in a way coming out of that."[5] You can feel it: the audience of several dozen artists, curators, scholars, and family members sitting on chairs, propped against the walls ("please don't touch the paintings," the moderator calls out), cross-legged on the floor, is silent, leaning forward and taking notes, thirsty and expectant for a road map for the personal-political of memory and its scalar translation into plastic form. And Unger delivers. But what strikes me are the two visual references I see, but that Unger does not mention in this moment of the talk, nor does Brenson's account of the work's first public presentation. And that is the debt of influence *Supplicant* owes in its scale, texture, and front-vertical orientation to spiritual artifacts of the Yombe peoples of the Kongo, especially minkisi and the wood, glass, and kaolin figures of nursing mothers and children. It was at this moment I realized that Unger's "sampling" from cultural referents and her study of the visual cultures of sacred motherhood across religious communities prefigured her well-known work on migration.

In her sketchbooks from the 1990s, Unger used the phrase the "Mary Problem" to denote both the singular form of the visual trope of mother with child and the postmodern sculptor's dilemma of how to "abstract" or essentialize such a multicultural phenomenon and still have the referent remain legible (figs. 4.2–4.10). The iconic triangular composition of mothers with young children—nursing, or held in arms, or both—is ubiquitous throughout history. It is not exclusive to the peoples of the Kingdom of Kongo nor to

Christian Europe. But the uplifted, outward orientation of the head away from the child, in conversation with the viewer, as well as the bare and pert geometric breasts are distinctly from the Yombe group of the Kongo people and have been sampled and remixed for centuries, most notably in the mid-1940s and into the 1950s with the bullet bra, and by Jean Paul Gaultier's ruched-velvet cone dress and the leather bustier costumes for Madonna's 1989–91 Blond Ambition tour. (The semiotic pun that it is a "Madonna" that brings this bust-form back into visual culture should be lost on no one.) In her drawings from 1990, one sees Unger "working out" the problem of abstracting the abstraction that is Mary and sacred motherhood; in her sketches, Unger thinks through Western and non-Western icons to come to the powerful elongated beams and piers that will characterize her formal language.

Minkisi, the plural form of n'kisi, translated as spirit, are often called "power figures" in Europe and the Americas, but they are much more nuanced and constitute only a small fraction of the variety of spiritual instruments employed among the peoples of the Kongo. In response to particular problems and health concerns,

> a Kongo priest would assemble particular recipes of medicines that were believed to draw a force. These were housed within a receptacle of some kind. Sometimes the priest would commission a sculptural form to play that role, and in those cases there was a dialogue between a sculptor and a priest. Both of them contributed their expertise to the efficacy of such instruments of power.[6]

Both these sculptural forms—the Christian Madonna and the Yombe n'kisi—elucidate and perform profound cultural work at the level of individual households and in larger society. Scholars believe that during the eighteenth and nineteenth centuries, as the centuries-old relationship between the Kingdom of Kongo and European principalities began to hinge on the slave

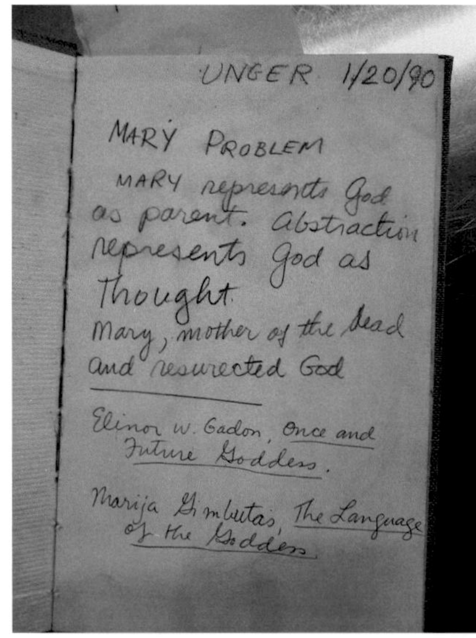

UNGER 1/20/90

MARY PROBLEM
MARY represents God
as parent. Abstraction
represents god as
Thought.
Mary, mother of the dead
and resurected God

Elinor W. Gadon, Once and
Future Goddess.

Marija Gimbutas, The Language
of the Goddess

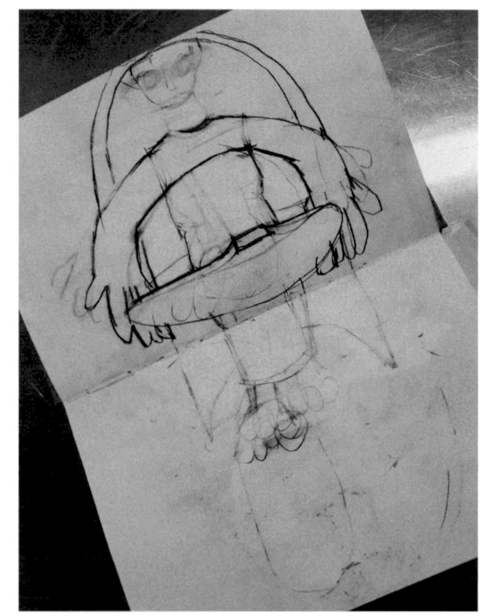

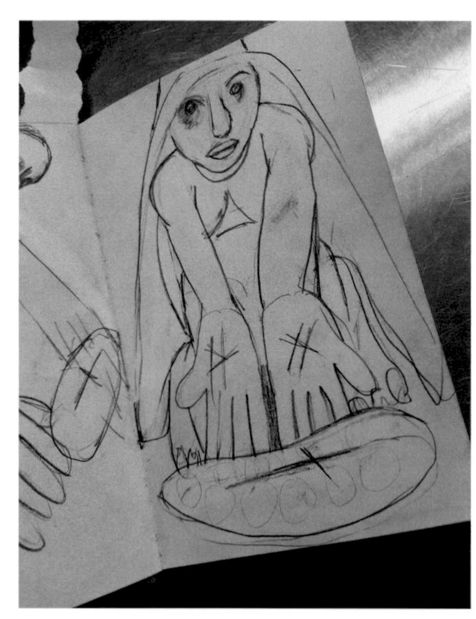

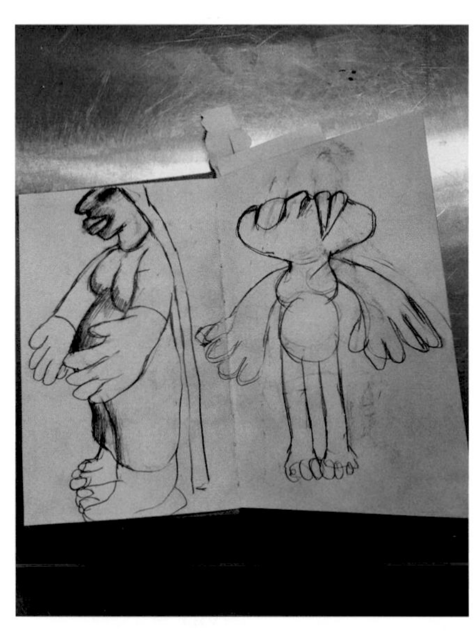

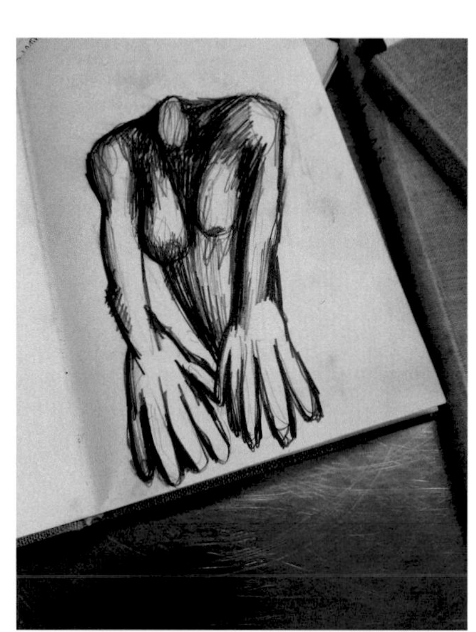

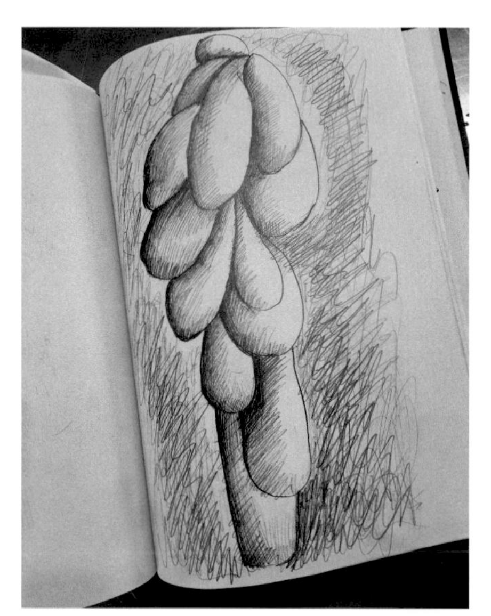

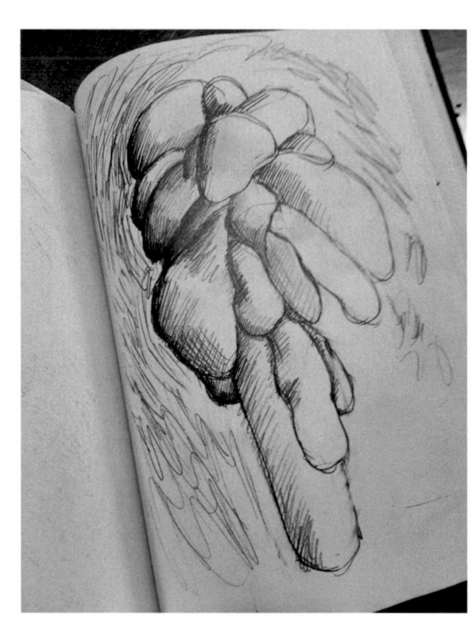

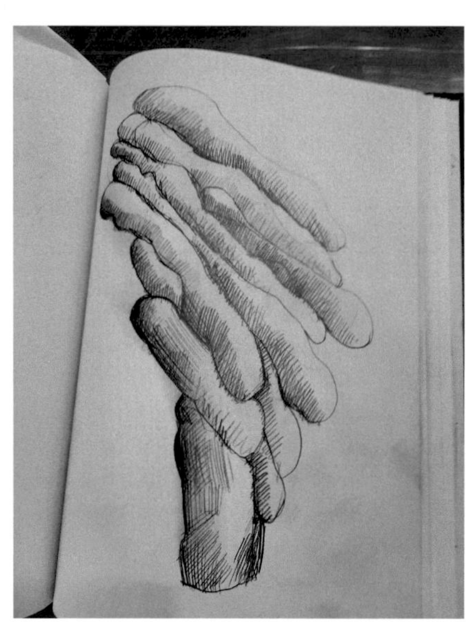

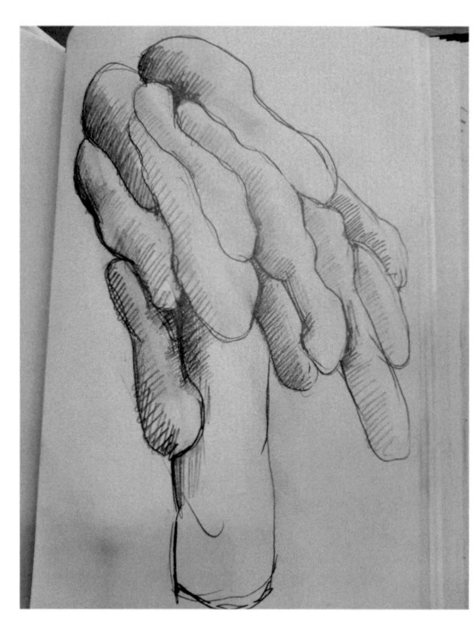

trade that was devastating the population of the kingdom, *minkondi*, a more aggressive and decidedly male styling of minkisi, became prominent. Meanwhile, the mother-with-child group became increasingly expressive in the figures' facial features and the weary droop of their shoulders and arm muscles as the scene the group represented became equally as aspirational as it was reflective of life's cycle. In this sense, amid the growing threat of globalization and colonial rule, these two distinct sculptural forms began to compress upon each other, animated by similar losses, and amplifying both familial spiritual concerns and a cultural need for community revitalization and reckoning.

The questions Eve Biddle initiated years before return. Is this an instance of aesthetic appropriation? If not, where is the line between appropriation and inspiration? If so, how much "research" do we expect artists to do? And what, if any, is the difference between appropriation in the era of smartphones and Google and the social media visual scandal, and in 1985, when the work was made, versus 1994, when the work was being discussed publicly as a conduit through which other works by the artist refer?

I confess that while I believe these questions are important, I do not find them that interesting. The more intriguing proposition, to me, the meatier and messier of intellectual quandaries to try and parse out, comes once we say, *Yes, sure, this is appropriative*. And then we ask, *Why?* What if, instead of asking in a post-Pop, post-DJ-sampled-hook world, *Did this artist appropriate?,* we ask, *To what end? And, What is the aesthetic significance and the cultural purpose and impact of their translation?*

The field of American art is having a moment of reckoning, and we come to Unger and her references in that moment. It is a moment of inflection and revision that will lead (let us pray) to redefinition. The trope of "portraits of white people painted by white people on white walls" is being seen for the constructed lie and sham that it is. I locate myself in this moment as a curator of American art who enjoys and seeks out multicultural and multidisciplinary references and

who questions the efficacy of "American" as a discourse.

I am also animated in my looking by the methodologies of comparative literature and religion (the disciplines I trained in before art history) where we examine texts through the lens of other texts. In my prior life, I did not call, for example, the Renaissance "discovery" of medieval Sufi astrology and medicine or Jewish philosophy and architectural innovation during the Roman empire "appropriation." I called it revelation, epiphany, reclamation, regain(ing), interpolation, and diachronic dialogue. Part of this was my youth and naivete. Part of it was my understanding that if these works had not been "found" or rediscovered, we may not have the works of al-Farabi, Ibn Sina (Avicenna), al-Kindi, Maimonides, and Paquda today. This is not to suggest that appropriation only occurs at the level of the visual or the glib. But I do think asking the reasons *why* a visual artist chooses to leverage certain cultural forms is more important than asking *if*.

I am reminded of Sanford Biggers's recent articulations and installations around the use and co-option of ethnographic subjects and religious iconography and his assertion that, in a vibrant conceptual practice, "all bets are off."[7] Unger, admittedly, is not as cavalier. And while I believe Unger's *Supplicant* (alongside other important works by her hand) to be appropriative, I do not think this is irredeemable, nor do I think she intended to instigate d.r.a.m.a. I think her choices of citation stand in powerful witness to the vibrant and continuous influence of African and Asian diasporas in the aesthetic imaginaries of the Americas, influences Unger encountered directly in her travels and her training. But the work of clarifying and reckoning with her choices must be done. The posthumous survey exhibition this publication supports does this work as it widens the circle of the ongoing dialogue Geoffrey Biddle began with me years before.

My words are meant not to offer prescription and stances but to open up nuanced positions and material approaches to Unger's practice, particularly the large-scale, engaged-to-the-wall sculptural installations

4.2–4.10
Phone images of Mary Ann Unger's 1990 sketchbook, in which she works out the "Mary Problem" across consecutive pages. Photos by Horace D. Ballard.

of her last years. I time travel lyrically, but I hope pointedly, in order to shape one of the key critical questions of any scholarly attention to Unger's practice—namely, the fluidity of resonances and inspirations from cultures both known to her and separate from her.

Sculpture is a practice of language in three dimensions, with a history and tradition that is multicultural and mutable across materials. Thus, I find it helpful to view appropriations and accretions with the same intention and emphasis as we might view the slippage of a word from one language system into another—not for the purposes of making light of appropriation, but being authentic to its commonplace-ness and its effects within the medium.

In researching Mary Ann Unger's life and in learning how transformative the year 1985, and *Supplicant* in particular, was for her practice, I cannot help but recall another monumental and magnificent work from 1985: Elaine Scarry's *The Body in Pain: The Making and Unmaking of the World*, in which Scarry famously declares, "What is remembered in the body is well remembered. It is not possible to compel a person to unlearn."[8] As humans, we are accustomed to the wound: first, a kind of glint or glitch intervention into or against the body by a foreign object; the smarting, the extraction, the bubbled-over russe and bloodbloom of experience; and then, cicatrix over cicatrix in formation, aided by bandaging. The scar offers futurities of grandeur: context and the promise of a story to tell.

But what happens when the wound is cancer: an exuberance of the cells themselves? What happens when the body, the divine system of organs and urges that once was capacious enough to produce life, is now hungry for its own death? How to proceed in praise and wonder of life, when the cicatrices form a chain-link fence of finality: subdividing one's organs into tessellated pastures sold off to pay a mortgage to God with terms you did not agree to? How to fight when the therapies of warfare cannot promise victory—but only IF you survive—that you will inhabit a new body lassoed and ransomed into a new gender? Ovid and T. S. Eliot tell us that even

Tiresias tired of being Tiresias, present for Neptune's rise and Phoebus's descent to collaborate on the building, and now the fall, of the sculpted walls of Troy. Even in the daily, slowish progression of old age, humans do not recognize the creatures they grow into. How to speak, then, how to describe, how to visualize the fears and the hungers that are unique to us all, but do not originate within us? *How to create out of decreation?*

There is something particularly sculptural about the quandary at the heart of my looking at and writing about Mary Ann Unger (fig. 4.11). The work of her hands affects me as that of few artists working in sculpture manage to do. Textural, sensate, kinesthetic, performative. In attending to Unger, I realize that sculpture is an attempt at a common language. To encounter Unger's work is to be compelled to language, verbal, gestural, written. The artist Phyllida Barlow is known for saying that sculpture-as-language "is about all kinds of longings: the longing to touch; the longing to walk around and still engage." Barlow's words resonate deeply. Sculpture has always seemed to me an invitation into pure presence, when, as Barlow indicates, the body and senses are reacting/relating and finding commonality: "It's not just 100% visual."[9] These words were in mind as I gazed around the room at works by Unger for the first time, in April 2018. Some freestanding, some engaged to the walls, some resting into one another. The air that held Biddle and me and the works was vibrating. The only way I know how to phrase it is to express that the objects contained and conveyed their own power.

Sometimes the answer to "How to create out of decreation?" is to reorient one's sense of what it means to create and find another language for one's situation. The search for a common visual language that holds diachronic sensations of past, present, future was alluring for Unger as both a thought exercise and, increasingly, as a response to her own situation of changing capacity and dis-ease. My aim is to be clear and explicit as to the artist's process, as well as the resultant stakes for both the viewer and the work. I am not justifying appropriative modalities, but having spent

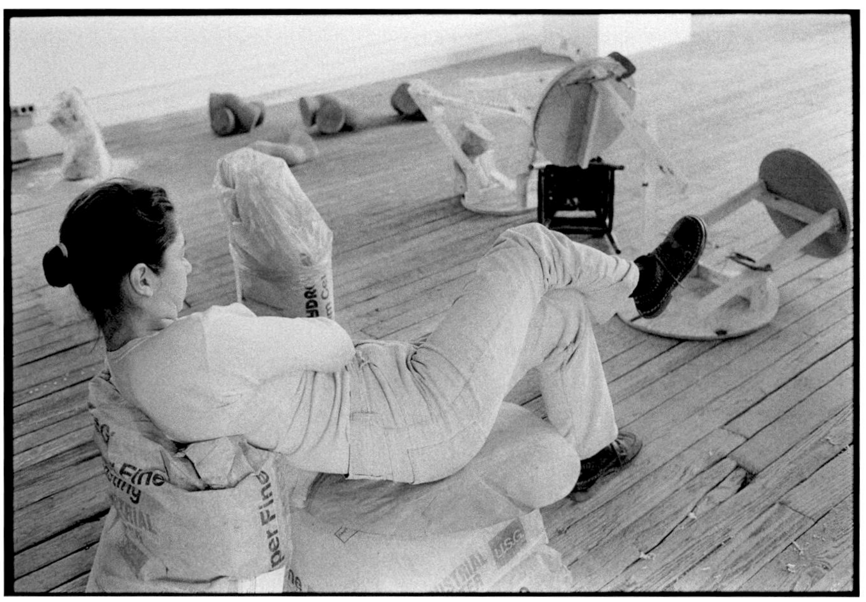

4.11
Mary Ann Unger, Third Street, New York, 1976. Photo by Geoffrey Biddle. Courtesy of the artist.

most of my career considering the conventions and formulations of modern portraiture in Europe and the Americas, I am interested in opening up Unger's contexts and thought processes around citation in ways that lead to greater appreciation of her complex typographies and forms.

Let's rejoin the artist's talk. Unger has just intoned, "*Next slide, please.*"

> As one gets further away from an experience, I think one is better able to communicate something. That's kind of strange about communication and abstraction. . . . This is a Guardian figure [now titled *Guardian of Music* (fig. 4.12)], it's also obviously a fertility image, and its direct inspiration was from an African instrument that I saw at the collection of instruments at the Met. It's a very small lute with a curved neck, and then these [indicates nodules along the vertical "neck" of the object] would be like the tuning keys, the breasts, and obviously it's like a flask, a container, but it does come out of the same piece with the four-stacked breasts.[10]

Geoffrey Biddle confirms that he and Unger often visited the Michael C. Rockefeller Collection at New York's Metropolitan

Museum of Art, "and we loved it." His memories build upon what has been explored elsewhere in this volume: that Unger's deep appreciation for the spiritually resonant and potent sculptural works of West Africa as well as the Sahara region, the Levant, and South America, emerged from the elastic capacities of an adept mind trained to find equivalence. Her skills at adapting and compressing several different cultural forms into an essentialized module became a methodological tool emerging from her academic training, as well as from her travels and her later use of imposed grids. But perhaps what is most insightful about Biddle's reminiscences is the sense that Unger saw no hierarchies between the great historic and ethnographic collections in the city's museums and the works on view in downtown galleries and regional sculpture parks. "We went often to all of them," Biddle writes.[11]

In *Supplicant*, I argue, Unger is building upon her training with the sculptor Minoru Niizuma at Columbia University and compressing multiple conscious and unconscious references into an abstracted—but still referential—power object, imbued with energy, expression, and the power of painful transformations of the body and of self/spirit/soul. In so doing, the knotted absurdity/precarity of life and illness get transmuted into the transformative leap Daphne takes to escape the love of Apollo (note the incongruent but still brilliant play between sun-lover and cancer here for a sense of Unger's deep-dark humor). As Daphne's bones and sinew turn, mid-jump, into laurel leaves, Unger-as-sculptor and Unger-as-survivor-fighter-of-illness meet in the negative but potent space at the margin, on the edge of sculpture and skin, which is both Søren Kierkegaard's *Glaubenssprung* (leap of faith in the face of life's absurdity) and the new world of Ovid's mythic possibility. Here, in this new state of metamorphosis, a renewed creature, both human and other, Daphne-as-Unger, needs a new and visible language. And so, Unger pulls from the part of the world that the Greeks believed Africa to be: το σπίτι του Απόλλωνα, the House of Apollo, and crafts for herself wings.

Something similar, if more legible, is happening in *Guardian of Music*. Here, a West African kora creates an elegant formal bridge from Unger's embodied, figurative circumstance (Jean-Paul Sartre would say, situation) to a form both specific and universal to those who tell stories and convey the epics of individuals and civilizations that *go through an experience drawing them into darkness and find their way out of it*.

Unger is moving not in co-option, but in analogy. The rounded, hollow body (a calabash) attached to a vertical spine, stick, or cord, with accompanying strings of various lengths and tensions that can be tuned to produce pleasing sound, recalls both a lute and a harp in its tonality. The kora is an instrument that, like the harp and oud, has ancient and contemporary transnational histories. In the years before her cancer diagnosis, and in the intervening years of the late 1980s and early '90s, Unger was in search of formal synergies that convey long(er) histories of pain, maternal intuition, and resilience than the art and artifacts the traditional Euro-American canon in the postmodern milieu can provide. Unger was not hoping to pick up the mantle of these forms and cultures. To my eye, she was reaching out, through the experience of pain and the greater capacities of empathy, which illness and pain leave in their wake, to find not just greater appreciation but formal resonance enough to inspire her to make anew.

Let's take a step back and zoom out and approach the slippage of appreciation, appropriation, exploitation, and inspiration on a macro-historical level. Since the era when Egyptian and Nubian gold, spices, grain, and terracotta bolstered the coffers and the estates of the Roman Empire in the third century BCE, and truly even before the time of Cleopatra and Caesar, the "Western" world has always appreciated and appropriated African, Oceanic, and continental Indigenous art, resources, myth, spiritual practices, and artisanal objects.

It happened to the Etruscan and Greek gods through the interpolative means of the *interpretatio romana*. Zeus became Jupiter. Athena became Minerva. (Oddly, Apollo remains Apollo, and Phoebus is actually another sun deity who occurs later. The geo-racial constructions of Apollo and his harp are fascinating when viewed through this fact.) The ancient mind knew this. The medieval mind knew this. Those who saw the retinue of the Christian ambassador from the kingdom of Arda in present-day Benin knew this, as did those who saw how warmly Louis XIV welcomed him and the treaty that ensured and insured marble and timber beams and gold and glass for Versailles in its early years. But those of us living in the centuries after the Enlightenment have either forgotten how connected and fluid the world has always been or are so Eurocentric as to feel a bit left out of histories that predate transatlantic colonial plunder.

Much has been written about the circumstances and the effects on modern art of Constantin Brancusi's 1922 visit to the Colonial Exposition in Marseilles and Pablo Picasso seeing a Gabonese Fang mask on the wall of André Derain's Montmartre studio. These are often seen as moments of cultural exploitation. A bit less (but no less importantly) has been written and discussed on the encounter between John Keats and the so-called Elgin or Parthenon marbles, taken from Athens by Thomas Bruce, 7th Earl of Elgin, between 1801 and 1805. A growing awareness is dawning of the importance of the encounter between a Vili n'kisi votive in a shop window and Henri Matisse in the rue de Rennes. These moments have largely been viewed through the lens of cultural dominance or exchange.

It is not the act of taking inspiration from the best and the most visually arresting of another culture that is dangerous. No. It is the sense that in having appreciated and been inspired, the borrowing individual or nation is now the benefactor, the expert, the holder, the owner, the genius,

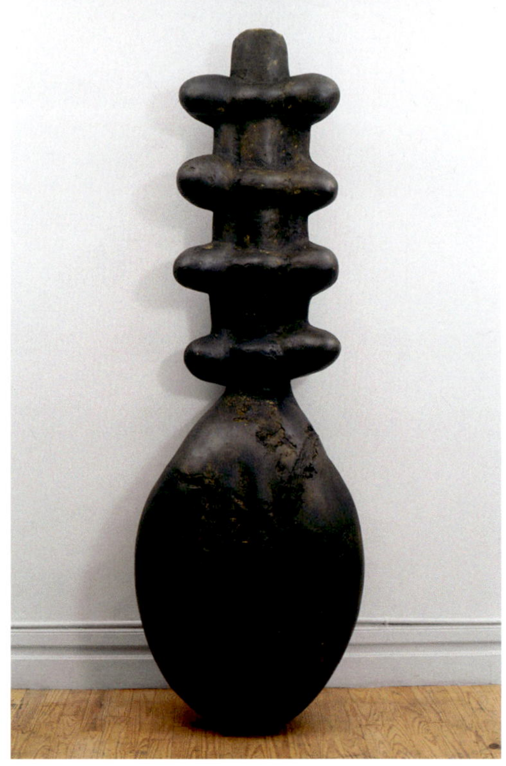

　Ballard

the advocate, the advancer, the beneficiary of that knowledge or style. It is the sense that in having been taken, the image is now "new," rather than introduced or translated. In aesthetic terms, the *longue durée* of a motif or material in one culture gets flattened into the moment of its "arrival" into the discourse of another. This forced removal and resettlement of a motif, object, practice, or idea is extraction.

Extraction begets the harm of erasure and the crime of revision without citation, by which appreciation and inspiration become exploitative appropriation. The dread deed occurs when intersectional, diachronic, longitudinal development in one culture heralds an ahistoric vanguard in another culture. It also occurs when emblems of power and mystery in one culture become decorative and ubiquitous in another. Plagiarism is the rupture. Flattening is the rupture. Claiming ownership over and "siting" a concept or motif that is atmospheric, deep, and endemic to human life is the rupture. And it is a deeply modern wound. Because as time has gone on, more and more governments, artists, and thinkers have seemed to fail to give credit, dismissing their source material as primitive, as ur-texts or paratexts with sensory resonance but no direct correlation or correspondence. Or, even worse, they couch exploitation as transitive apologetics, stating that an idea or conceit began in one place, but was "perfected" and "leveraged appropriately" by another that "knew the value." Syncretic absorption and the creation of hybridized cultures is human, mutable, mutual. Appropriation is a tool of conquest.

Back to Unger. What I find intriguing is that the impulse for Unger's particular appropriative act feels so different from the examples and histories above, and also feels different from the glut of appropriations during her own cultural moment. Andy Warhol's *The Last Supper* aside, the artists of Pop and its second wave (for example, Jean-Michel Basquiat, Roy Lichtenstein, Gronk, Keith Haring, Ann Hamilton, Yayoi Kusama, David Hockney, Monchi, Nayland Blake, Wayne Thiebaud, la Warhol, etc.) and the artists of the Pictures Generation (for example, Barbara Kruger, Cindy Sherman, Sherri Levine, Jack Goldstein, John Baldessari, Barbara Bloom, Richard Prince, Laurie Simmons, Robert Longo, etc.) are largely appropriating images from their own moment, or at least images created and circulated in their lifetimes, and repurposing images as a way of (re)positioning disillusionment and institutional critique as endemic structures of American decline. These artists, in a sense, were reselling "America" back to itself: reframing and repackaging the commercialized pastiche of consumerism.

Unger is not doing this. She is treading waters more akin to the *personal-is-political* rather than the Pictures Generation's sense of *misogyny + the white male gaze = a tax on culture none of us can afford* and *consumerism + blithe participation in capitalist entertainment = death of self and the decline of Western culture*. (All three of which are 100 percent true, by the way.)

Nor are Unger's inspirations and conflations rising (for me) to the level of Dana Schutz's notorious *Open Casket* (2016), which sparked art-world conversations around appropriation during and after the 2017 Whitney Biennial. Regardless of Schutz's intentions, there was a gap between those artistic concerns and the visceral antipathy and cultural riposte to the reception of her act of borrowing the brutalized image of Emmett Till.[12] This gap is called implicit bias. Especially in a moment when Black bodies in duress and in moments of entering their mortality are being streamed, are going viral, and the world watches, and nothing in the past five years—or fifty years—seems to have changed all that much. What this raises for me are the nuances around what is considered "public domain," by which I mean, in polite society (Is the art world "polite"? Unclear.), who has the "right" or, more precisely, the moral authority to speak upon, and thus to act alongside, and in the stead of, certain histories and images?

It is this sense of transcultural evidence and of human memory, not just images, not just objects and ways of approaching form and meaning, but *history*, that I wish to return to for the remainder of our conversation.

When we look across Unger's body of work, it is in her last years of making, when the work is at its most abstract and furthest removed from the referent of the body, that I find not its forms, per se, but the artist's language around its formal conception the most disconcerting—and thus, for our purposes, the worthiest of attention.

Let's once more rejoin the artist's talk. Unger has again intoned, *"Next slide, please."*

> All of these pieces that you're going to see, more or less, are made out of Hydrocal over welded steel armature and the armature underneath these is actually a grid. It's a grid made out of eight-inch welding rods so that my initial interaction with the piece is actually very delicate.[13]

The grid in Western art: a tool of compartmentalization and of distancing; a visible method of comparison and analysis, of positions and impositions, of defining typologies and persons/forms that are "irregular." The grid is loaded. Even in the rigorous and novel ways by which Unger constructs her hexagonal and trigonal supra-imposed grids, they are still grids. Even though one can argue (as I have argued) that Unger's gridded impositions give permission for her to decenter Western notions of scale; to seek a new understanding of "finished" surface; and dismiss symmetrical radial axis in favor of more lateral, intuitive knotted and biomorphic configurations of space. Even with the frankly enchanting disjuncture of the haptic delicacy of metal rod in Unger's palm, we must come to pause. The grid can only be delicate, universal, for a very select few. For the majority of the world, the grid is indistinguishable from loaded histories of colonization and racist hegemonies of order that connote the sense that if the "right" formula can be deduced, the world can be "mapped" and "known."

Around the same time as the 1994 artist talk that commenced our discussion, Unger wrote two different artist's statements about the work that is widely viewed to be her masterpiece. Around thirty-four elements—lintels or open palms approximately two to five feet in height, and posts of approximately ten to fourteen feet in length—spread in "variable size and configuration" across an expanse of space, mimetic of walking, crossing, "mothers holding their children, men carrying their dead," toward a goal. In progress during her year as a Guggenheim Fellow in 1992, the work titled *Across the Bering Strait* "is about migration" and "refers to the Mongol migration across the land bridge known as Beringia, between Asia and Alaska."[14]

Throughout the various statements, Unger's language regarding her own work and its concerns with histories she knows and histories she has researched strike me as matter-of-fact, well researched, and reflective. There's singular beauty in the modular topographies of form Unger has invented for herself that give expressive force to her own embodied pain and the crossing of "polar space… the limit of both empire and human experience":[15] torso-like structures that redouble as upheld arms and cusping palms, as well as open mouths in prayer, in song, in mid-scream. Unger believes deeply in the power and intentions of the work but does not take herself too seriously. We can look behind us/her and see the reference to *Supplicant* and also note the growth of the artist-as-human years later. All to the good.

But there are also moments, especially when it concerns familial histories, that I find disconcerting as they blur oral tradition with self-effacement and caricature. In a first-person artist statement, Unger sets to language the visual and emotive memory of her paternal grandmother, "sensitive, very sweet, and perhaps too delicate…. she died young. I have always associated her with a deep melancholy and with a connection to the unconscious, which is manifested in my work." This generous preamble of an approach into Unger's practice is laid side-by-side on the page with the artist's invocation of the "primeval histories" of the Mongol migration across Eurasia into the Americas with multiple threads of the Jewish Diaspora, and a father reportedly "descended from Atilla the Hun," due to his dark coloring and phenotypical features. In the weave of all these authentic and potential selves, Unger positions *Across the Bering Strait* as a sculpted, semimiraculous "personal mythology that symbolically unifies the disparate origins of this country."[16] This statement is perhaps the most appropriative gesture Unger enacts. It is not without a kind of merit. It emerges from a real place and a real political hope, even yearning, for more unity, perhaps even equity. But we are not there yet. And this language is not there yet.

I realize the artist statement, like the curatorial label, is a particular form of expression. It is (necessarily) a compressed and condensed space of explication and meaning. Fair enough.

But in a separate, third-person statement, Unger describes a sound component of the work, drawn from recordings of "Tibetan ritual chants, eskimo vocal games, and Inuit Indian chants." Activated by these sourced sounds, an "inherently dramatic" abstract work "about migration" becomes a configuration of elements, with each piece of the assembled "players in a performance."[17] (Oof.) Reading Unger's words nearly thirty years after she wrote them is an uncanny exercise. The structural possibilities of the artist's verve and vision are startling, bold, and exciting. The tone of the language and the alacrity of connections give pause. For amid these vignettes and family histories that form (for Unger) a sensorium heady enough to evoke historical and present migrations, is a foghorn for the contemporary reader, punctuating just how close we are to the precipice of cultural appropriation and the roiling sea of stereotype, without the sense of personal-cultural exchange and fluency that Unger so generously expressed in *Supplicant* and *Guardian of Music*.

For our exhibition in 2022, the museum and the Unger Estate are addressing appropriation and citation head-on. When we install *Across the Bering Strait*, we will engineer a way that Unger's intended sound accompaniment can activate the piece at certain times. We will address the sound component in our interpretive materials. We will organize decided and conscientious programming that leverages the sound component as a way of engaging the various histories and connotations raised in this essay. We even hope to commission new sounds, by students and community members, that are reflective of their individual sensory responses to the themes of migration, displacement, diaspora, and cultural memory.

But for the majority of the work's installation, *Across the Bering Strait* will be sotto voce. We do this because we have evidence that during her life, Unger displayed elements and passages of the work without sound. We also believe Unger's vision to be so powerful that the work (though it, of course, is contoured by sound) loses nothing if this singular component is estranged. We do this as an instance of practical pedagogy in contemporary curatorial practice. A work changes over time. The reception and interpretation of works of art change over time. A work of art should stand the test of time. All three things are true.

For some, this may not be enough. For some, Unger may be ripe for "canceling." But that seems too easy and too blunt a tool—even spurious. I think we lose more than is gained. Unger was trying to offer space to the descendants of peoples whose migration sparked the origins of pre-Columbian civilizations and whose audacity was the genesis of a work of art. It may be a bit mawkish, on the nose, or clunky. But there was great effort, and her perceived connection to migration in her own ancestry was real.

When we police appropriation and "cancel" artists, I think we foreclose the possibility of real human connection and inclination toward knowing and the making of new meanings and new histories through blended experience. Homi K. Bhabha's notion of hybridity and the creation of "third space" may emerge for some here.[18] I do not interrogate it here, as I have no sense at this moment that Unger read Bhabha, Gayatri Chakravorty Spivak, or Edward Said. I also think we arrive at the train station without them, as it were. However, I do think that postcolonial studies as a discipline and a field of critique raises up the provocative and poignant inability for any of us, in the "West," to move outside the cultural imperialism of our own positionalities. For us, there must always be an "Orient" to be "oriented" toward and against. Inspiration is never pure. To believe so is to believe the worst of all the lies of white supremacy. I began by stating that it is not the act of appropriation I find interesting enough to debate, but rather the reasons why an artist makes that choice.

In the early days of exhibition planning, a wonderful colleague with whom I discussed the broad circumference of Unger's practice reminded me that artists in the Western world are "heir to two phenomenological expressions of human experience since the Renaissance."[19] On the one hand is the discourse of humanism and its attendant preoccupations with reason, that ineffable, invisible, seemingly divine force that can only be gleaned (supposedly) through the ideal (white) form (and, hence, preoccupations with superiority). The other expression is the "*mechanique*, that decidedly modern, component-based auto-invention wherein material sleekness, sheen and geometric parts in-form and propel the speed and frequency of modern life." Sensual excess and perfection on one hand, economy and consistency and forward motion on the other. My colleague's words were galvanizing. Now I could envision the process, or problem, of bringing essential human archetypes into form—into what Adrienne Rich phrases as "the dream of a common language"[20]—that has preoccupied artists across time and place and medium. The work of art that aggregates forms and textures and scale to engender a mood powerful enough to affect the viewer over time must be imbued with a kind of insight into its own time that is at once specific and contextual. The interrogation between hand and material must be immediate enough to be legible across time, but instinctive enough to be yummy, touchable, desirable, and desirous to future selves and future audiences.

Unger's desire to create encounters pregnant with sensuous connections to life meant that she had to look beyond years of acculturation in an academic praxis that prized the editing of form and the rigors of fabrication. She had to probe the ontological question of being. She had to ask about, and pull into the visible world, the archetypes of warmth, warning, and wary and weary love that have sustained and touched every human life. Ambitious, yes. But nothing is more personal or political than archetypes: those visible forms that strive toward the impossibility of universality. And so, Unger moved, not in comparison but in analogy. Rather than laying claim to histories and rituals not her own, she was finding in them emotional and intuitive connective tissue for her own experience, her own working through of self and her collective identities of being a woman, of being a mother, of being a Jew, of being an artist, of being one stricken with a chronic illness with a lessening control, day by day, over the self. She was not conquering, but she was calling into being a kind of fluency between inspiration and meaning that is worth detangling.

All histories are partial. Colonization is not the only force that fragments and imposes arbitrary and hierarchical structures on the world. There is no need to weaponize decolonialist frameworks against Mary Ann Unger. The artist is not performing colonial extraction. Unger (here) is *not* not citing her sources. And yet. Her inspirations are multicultural and removed from contemporary politics, permitting a slippage between place, time, material, form, and meaning.

There is a historical gap in her attentions that can be read as naive at best, conflating and surface at worst. Honest critique can be raised. Still, it is important to position this aspect of her practice within a larger configuration of history and influence and material. It is also important, I suggest, to think about the formation of a practice in-becoming, and, critically, the reasons *why*…

Unger rejected Minimalist lexicons in an effort to create and refine a unique conceptual language that accords with the mimetic, modular, and mutable semiotics of great sculpture. Her works, as she defined them, constitute a varied range of power objects: fetish forms if you like. Across three distinct works, we have seen how Unger displaced power onto and into vertical and lateral

Ballard

forms—and even, perhaps, formed newly empowered bodies and alter/altar-selves, forms with almost-sentient animus and energetic conductivities in their relation to spaces, histories, and viewers. These are not reliquaries, nor are they horcruxes or minkisi. These are analogies and correlations. They are transitive thought experiments at their best. Unger is doing soul work in the midst of personal transition, and that means her practice accrues patterns, totems, and possibilities.

If one wishes to do sculptural work that draws the empirical experience of pain and change into the figurative, but does not veer into the terrain (per Aria Dean, John Solt, and Daniel Trilling) of "cannibalizing biography" or excoriating one's own archive (for that would best be performed in a different genre of expression), where does one look? One looks to myth; one looks, I think, to shapes, to vessels, and other containers and conditions of power. The body becomes a semiotic footnote to the foregrounded texture of a form. Subjectivities are never obscured, but they are, like the grids, layered, rubbed up against, worn away by love and attention. The edges are ridged, pinched, probed… no smooth surfaces, no easy allusions. There is a seismic, multidimensional, biomorphic flow to Unger's work across genre and media. In order to grapple with how and why Unger translates such energies and ecologies of self from embodied memory into sculpted form, the relationship of sculpture to cultural appreciation-appropriation must be engaged.

To write about sculpture in the midst of a pandemic—when we cannot touch, when we cannot gather—adds to the longing and attendant restlessness of the medium. The medium's dual attentions, between verisimilitude and longing, situate sculpture as a common visual language beyond objecthood. If sculpture is about longing, it is also about dimensional memory. An artist can look at certain positions, facets, or passages of the sculpture and, as artist Rachel Feinstein perceives, "remember where they were and how it felt to make it." It does not seem improbable that Unger would have found truth in a recent reflection by Feinstein, who writes, "Sculptures are extensions of the body that do not age and decay with time like flesh does. Sculpture is the pathway I use to be immortal."[21]

There is nothing fragile or chill about Unger's work. It is all strength. It is all considered and decided. But there is a kind of restlessness, a question of whether something is ever fully finished, even if it is realized; it seems more correct to suggest that the works as we know them are intransitive and momentarily stopped, lingering with us: on pause, until we animate them with our own stories and meanings. The great tragedy and injustice of it all is that we are denied Unger in the twenty-first century. We are denied what comes next.

I close with Unger's own words—the words that initially led me to propose to organize her first solo museum presentation in over twenty years. Words that seem as appropriate and prophetic now as they did, I am sure, in the mid-1990s. Words that hold within them, like medicine, a prayer for possible futures:

Across the Bering Strait is about the past, but it is also about the present. Populations are shifting all over the world today, refugees from battle or oppression, hopeful immigrants and adventurers pursuing dreams. They carry their nationalities and their cultures with them just as they carry their possessions. We may have our hopes for an information superhighway and our dreams of an interconnected world in the technological twenty-first century, yet it is still the movements of peoples that makes us aware of each other around the world: migration is arguably the strongest force towards the creation of a global village. Just as it made the world larger thirty thousand years ago, it is still people moving, migrating, and even literally walking, that is making the world smaller [and, dare I add, more united] today.[22]

Notes

1. The story of art doyenne Laura Whitman Williams '89 and her annual winter cocktail party for the friends of the Williams College Museum of Art (WCMA) is legendary. It was Laura who first introduced me to Eve Biddle, and for that—and for all she has given in support of WCMA—she has my admiration and gratitude.

2. There was no resistance—neither in that first conversation nor in all the conversations that continue—to addressing the sticky places of Unger's practice. There was only trust, encouragement, and, where possible, a hope for the centering of Unger's own words. I am grateful for such time and such care and such trust. In the three years between that first meeting and the writing of this essay, I have come to the belief that Unger was reaching out in the position of an ally with "dreams of an interconnected world." See Mary Ann Unger, Guggenheim Artist Statement, 1992–95, n.p. I also believe that *Across the Bering Strait* and other sticky moments in her practice, twenty years on, traverse the cultural battlegrounds of cultural appropriation/appreciation and representational politics. Unger affords us a rich and singular vision through which we can examine and interrogate our times and our reactions. This is what I love about being a curator: the chance to engage work that presses on the cultural politics of its diachronic "moment": the moment of its making and the moment of its viewing.

3. Mary Ann Unger, in "Abstraction as a Timeless Art Form," Artists Talk on Art, panel moderated by Clement Meadmore, with John L. Moore, Robert Murray, Peter Stroud, Martin Bull, and Mary Ann Unger, Fulcrum Gallery, SoHo, January 21, 1994. Artists Talk on Art Records, circa 1974–2018, Archives of American Art, Smithsonian Institution.

4. Michael Brenson, "Art: Sculpture: 'Figure as Image of the Psyche,'" *New York Times*, November 8, 1985.

5. Unger, in "Abstraction as a Timeless Art Form."

6. Rachel High, "Great Traditions—*Kongo Power and Majesty* with Alissa LaGamma," Met Museum blogs, September 21, 2015, http://www.metmuseum.org/blogs/now-at-the-met/2015/great-traditions-kongo-power-and-majesty.

7. Sanford Biggers, quoted in Sarah Rose Sharp, "Sanford Biggers at MOCAD," *Detroit Art Review*, September 13, 2016, http://detroitartreview.com/2016/09/sanford-biggers-mocad/.

8. Elaine Scarry, *The Body in Pain: The Making and Unmaking of the World* (London: Oxford University Press, 1985), 110.

9. @hauserwirth, "From her home studio in London, #PhyllidaBarlow talks to Jennifer Higgie about Giacometti, lockdown and the theater of sculpture…," Instagram, February 13, 2021, http://www.instagram.com/p/CLPE-NlgQdo/.

10. Unger, in "Abstraction as a Timeless Art Form."

11. The more fulsome quote: "We went often to all of them, bought catalogues, and really appreciated what those cultural institutions brought to our lives and to the life of the city. And we went to galleries too." Biddle also writes of a fascinating personal connection between him, and thus Unger, as his spouse, and the Rockefeller collection: "The Michael Rockefeller collection had an extra link for me, and for us, through my college teacher and New York City friend Richard Rogers. He'd studied and then worked with the filmmaker Robert Gardner of *Dead Birds* fame. Michael Rockefeller, one year out of college, had been the sound man when *Dead Birds* was filmed, in 1960, and my friend Dick I think saw himself as a sort of compatriot of Michael, both young talents helping the older Gardner. Michael as you know went missing on a native artifacts acquisition expedition in 1961. Dick would joke about Michael's having been eaten because he was stealing/buying/removing sacred objects." Geoffrey Biddle to Horace Ballard, email correspondence, February 20, 2021.

12. See (for context) Randy Kennedy, "Painting of Emmett Till Draws Protests," *New York Times*, March 22, 2017; Jo Livingstone and Lovia Gyarkye, "The Case against Dana Schutz," *New Republic*, March 22, 2017, http://newrepublic.com/article/141506/case-dana-schutz; Ted Loos, "After the Quake, Dana Schutz Gets Back to Work," *New York Times*, January 9, 2019, http://www.nytimes.com/2019/01/09/arts/design/dana-schutz-painting-emmett-till-petzel-gallery.html.

13. Unger, "Abstraction as a Timeless Art Form."

14. Mary Ann Unger, Artist's Statement [third-person], "Across the Bering Strait," c. 1992–95, Mary Ann Unger Estate. Unger wrote two almost identical, undated artist's statements for *Across the Bering Strait*, both reproduced in this volume on pp. 86–87. The primary difference is in point of view: they include a first-person and a third-person treatment. For the purposes of clarity across the volume, the statements will be distinguished as such.

15. Jen Hill, *White Horizon: The Arctic in the Nineteenth-Century British Imagination* (Albany: SUNY Press, 2008), 3.

16. Mary Ann Unger, Artist's Statement [first-person], "Across the Bering Strait," c. 1992–95, Mary Ann Unger Estate.

17. Unger, Artist's Statement [third-person]. The desire to address in the text the harm of Unger's use of the term "eskimo" here with [sic] or additional language was strong. However, it felt best not to critique her usage of the racist

Ballard

anachronism specifically, but to address the times and the broader appropriation comprehensively, as the text does.

18. Homi K. Bhabha, *The Location of Culture* (London: Rutledge Classics, 1994).

19. I am indebted in this paragraph and throughout this essay to a conversation in October 2020 with the wonderful art historian and my dear colleague Michelle M. Apotsos, associate professor of art at Williams College, whom I quote here and below. She was there for me in a moment of intellectual need when I was elative and confused. I am forever grateful.

20. Adrienne Rich, *The Dream of a Common Language* (New York: W. W. Norton, 1978).

21. Rachel Feinstein, for *Stories: The Jewish Museum* blog, January 15, 2021, http://stories .thejewishmuseum.org/rachel-feinstein-discusses -maiden-mother-crone-7ca42535445a?gi =d9a2200ff8eb.

22. Unger, Artist's Statement [third-person].

MARY ANN UNGER

5 EAST 3RD STREET,   NEW YORK, N.Y.   10003   212-505-7713

ACROSS THE BERING STRAIT

"Across the Bering Strait" is an abstract sculpture about migration. It is an installation of variable size and configuration, always on the theme of movement in one direction, always suggesting people walking, carrying, in limbo but moving towards a goal.

The title refers to the Mongol migration across the land bridge which existed, by most recent estimates, twenty-nine thousand years ago between Asia and what is now Alaska, a migration which spread throughout the American continents.*   It evokes memories of our primeval history and suggests a continuity between the journeys of our ancestors and our personal journey. For Unger, whose grandparents include Russian and Hungarian Jews, one particular reference is to the Diaspora.

The units are posts and lintels – uprights which transform themselves into figures marching across the gallery floor, endowing the work with a narrative content. They suggest migrants carrying their tent poles and their bundles of possessions on their shoulders. Though the forms are abstract, they have a distinctly figurative aspect.   The posts are torsolike, whereas the lintels are limblike.   "Across the Bering Strait" suggests migrants carrying their tent poles and their bundles of possessions on their shoulders.   It also suggests mothers holding their children, or men carrying their dead home from war.

The uprights measure from two to five feet high and the horizontals range in size from ten to fourteen feet long.   The forms are made of cement with an acrylic binder pressed into fiberglass cloth, molded over a welded steel armature.   Pigment is added to the cement either during the process or after.   The basic colors are black or grey with some ochres added as a wash on the surface.

There is music which accompanies the piece based on Tibetan ritual chants, eskimo vocal games, and Inuit Indian chants.   The sculpture is inherently dramatic, but with the addition of music, the pieces become players in a performance.

"Across the Bering Strait" is about the past, but it is also about the present.   Populations are shifting all over the world today, refugees from battle or oppression, hopeful immigrants and adventurers pursuing dreams. They carry their nationalities and their cultures with them just as they carry their possessions.   We may have our hopes for an information superhighway and our dreams of an interconnected world in the technological twenty-first century, yet it still the movements of peoples that makes us aware of each other around the world: migration is arguably the strongest force towards the creation of a global village. Just as it made the world larger thirty thousand years ago, it is still people moving, migrating, and even literally walking, that is making the world smaller today.

---

* It takes three years to walk from the western tip of Alaska to the southernmost tip of Chile, walking 12 miles a day.

Mary Ann Unger, Artist's
Statement [third-person],
"Across the Bering Strait,"
c. 1992–95. Courtesy of
the Mary Ann Unger
Estate.

ACROSS THE BERING STRAIT

"Across the Bering Strait" is an abstract sculpture about migration. It is an installation of variable size and configuration, always on the theme of movement in one direction, always suggesting people walking, carrying, in transit, but always progressing towards a goal.

The title refers to the Mongol migration across the land bridge known as Beringia, between Asia and Alaska. The bridge existed up until the last ten thousand years ago, and it made possible migration into and throughout the American continents* "Across the Bering Strait" evokes memories of our primeval history and suggests a continuity between the journeys of our ancestors and our journeys today. My paternal grandparents were Russian and Hungarian Jews, and for me one specific reference of the title is to the Diaspora.

My father's father was the Hungarian Jew, born on the Lower East Side. The earliest story I know about him is that at twelve, he made burglar alarms for his parents and neighbors by attaching live electricity to the door knobs of their apartments. He went on to be an inventor and businessman with over two hundred patents.

Mother always said that Dad was descended from Atilla the Hun. "You can tell by his heavy eyelids," she would say, and I imagined my ancestors roaring out of Asia across the great Russian steppes with fierce eyes, riding massive steeds. My father had a wonderful ability to do things in the real world: electricity, engineering, plumbing, carpentry, mathematics, gardening. I aspired to be like him.

My father's mother came from Russia as a very young girl. Her picture makes her look sensitive, very sweet, and perhaps too delicate. She longed to return to Russia, and she died young. I have always associated her with a deep melancholy and with a connection to the unconscious,   which is manifested in my work.

My forebears' trip to America was yet another journey in the saga of the wandering Jew. I feel great pride in the strength and perseverance of my Jewish ancestors, in their inventiveness and creativity, their respect for learning and education, and their ability to succeed in the face of great difficulties.

My mother's parents were Catholic immigrants who settled in Boston, one Irish and one Portuguese, and I feel that I am a true representative of America's melting pot. "Across the Bering Strait" presents a personal mythology that symbolically unifies the disparate origins of this country.

---

* It takes three years to walk from the western tip of Alaska to the southernmost tip of Chile, walking twelve miles a day.

Mary Ann Unger, Artist's Statement [first-person], "Across the Bering Strait," c. 1992–95. Courtesy of the Mary Ann Unger Estate.

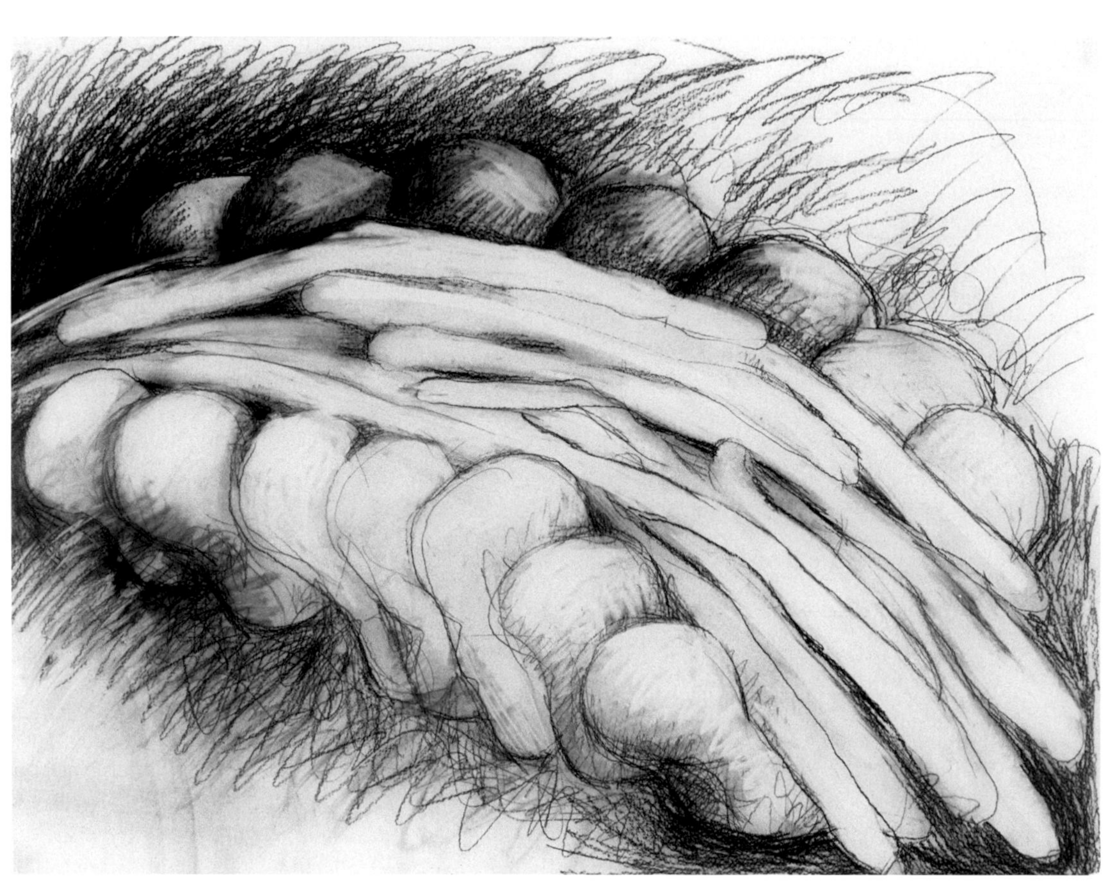

Checklist of the Exhibition

Mary Ann Unger: Dimensional Works

Untitled, 1975
Aluminum screen
29 × 27 × 5 in.
ID #0125
Mary Ann Unger Estate
Fig. 1.9

Benchmarks, 1977
Bonded iron
Each 42 × 21 × 19 in.
ID #4555
Mary Ann Unger Estate

Untitled, 1979
Aluminum screen
15 × 10 × 5 in.
ID #0136
Mary Ann Unger Estate

Untitled, 1979
Aluminum screen
20½ × 6½ × 2½ in.
ID #0138
Mary Ann Unger Estate

Untitled, 1979
Aluminum screen
40 × 16 × 6 in.
ID #0234
Mary Ann Unger Estate

Red Vertebrae, 1980
Painted plywood
(a): 20 × 12 × 15 in.
(b): 22⅝ × 12 × 14¹¹⁄₁₆ in.
(c): 26¹⁄₁₆ × 12 × 13⅝ in.
(d): 28⅜ × 12 × 11⅞ in.
(e): 30 × 12 × 11⅛ in.
Whitney Museum of
American Art, Gift of
Geoffrey Biddle,
2018.41a–e
Fig. 1.24

Supplicant, 1985
Hydrocal over steel with
pigment
45 × 48 × 36 in.
ID #7898
Mary Ann Unger Estate
Fig. 1.16

Guardian of Music,
1987–91
Hydrocal over steel with
pigment, wax, and
graphite
90 × 32 × 23 in.
Munson-Williams-
Proctor Arts Institute,
Gift of the artist, 98.9
Fig. 4.12

*Fragments Series,
No. 10*, 1990
Bronze
5½ × 3½ × 2¾ in.
ID #0034
Mary Ann Unger Estate

*Fragments Series,
No. 18 (Reach)*, 1990
Bronze
6¾ × 4 × 5½ in.
ID # 7736
Mary Ann Unger Estate

*Fragments Series,
No. 21 (Leonard
Bernstein)*, 1990
Bronze
6½ × 6 × 5 in.
ID #7739
Mary Ann Unger Estate

*Fragments Series,
No. 23*, 1990
Bronze
4 × 7 × 3 in.
ID #0047
Mary Ann Unger Estate

*Fragments Series,
No. 24*, 1990
Bronze
5¾ × 6 × 2½ in.
ID #0049
Mary Ann Unger Estate

*Fragments Series,
No. 29 (Woman
Walking)*, 1990
Bronze
5 × 7 × 4 in.
ID #0033
Mary Ann Unger Estate

*Fragments Series,
No. 31 (Man)*, 1990
Bronze
7½ × 6½ × 2¼ in.
ID #0046
Mary Ann Unger Estate

*Fragments Series,
No. 33 (Man Stretching)*,
1990
Bronze
7 × 8 × 2 in.
ID #0054
Mary Ann Unger Estate

*Fragments Series,
No. 35 (Man with Arms
Extended)*, 1990
Bronze
9 × 5 × 2 in.
ID #7745
Mary Ann Unger Estate

*Fragments Series,
No. 36 (Discus)*, 1990
Bronze
6 × 6 × 4½ in.
ID #0053
Mary Ann Unger Estate

*Fragments Series,
No. 39 (After Bacon)*,
1990
Bronze
5¼ × 6½ × 3½ in.
ID #0051
Mary Ann Unger Estate

*Fragments Series,
No. 43*, 1990
Bronze
8 × 5 × 4½ in.
ID #0045
Mary Ann Unger Estate

*Fragments Series,
No. 44*, 1990
Bronze
9 × 6 × 6 in.
ID #0039
Mary Ann Unger Estate

*Fragments Series,
No. Unknown*, 1990
Bronze
5 × 2½ × 2 in.
ID #0050
Mary Ann Unger Estate

Across the Bering Strait,
1992–94
Hydrocal over steel with
pigment and graphite
Multiple elements,
dimensions variable
Mary Ann Unger Estate
Figs. 3.1–3.4, 4.1

*Fragments Series,
No. 51*, 1993
Bronze
17 × 9½ × 3 in.
ID #0031
Mary Ann Unger Estate
Fig. 1.22

Ganesha, 1996–97
Hydrocal over steel with
pigmented patina
90 × 32 × 19 in.
ID #2344
Mary Ann Unger Estate

Shanks, 1996–97
Hydrocal and
cheesecloth over steel
armatures
109 × 98 × 34 in.
Williams College
Museum of Art,
Museum purchase,
Karl E. Weston Memorial
Fund, M.2020.16
Fig. 1.25

**Mary Ann Unger:
Works on Paper**

Untitled, 1976
Graphite on paper
30 × 22 in.
ID #0067
Mary Ann Unger Estate
Fig. 1.10

Benchmarks, 1977
Watercolor on paper
8 × 10 in.
ID #1494
Davidson Gallery

Benchmarks, 1977
Watercolor on paper
8 × 10 in.
ID #1496
Davidson Gallery

Untitled, 1977
Watercolor on paper
10½ × 7½ in.
ID #1498
Mary Ann Unger Estate

Untitled, 1977
Watercolor on paper
10½ × 7½ in.
ID #1499
Mary Ann Unger Estate

Untitled, 1978
Graphite on paper
22½ × 30 in.
ID #1089
Mary Ann Unger Estate

Untitled, 1978
Wax-graphite on
gessoed paper
22½ × 30 in.
ID #1094
Mary Ann Unger Estate

*Study for Hexagonal
Quintet #2*, 1978
Graphite on paper
22½ × 30 in.
ID #1098
Mary Ann Unger Estate

Untitled, 1978
Graphite on paper
22½ × 30 in.
ID #1101
Mary Ann Unger Estate

Untitled, c. 1978
Graphite on paper
22½ × 30 in.
ID #1105
Mary Ann Unger Estate

Untitled, 1978
Wax-graphite on
gessoed paper
22 × 30 in.
ID #1121
Mary Ann Unger Estate

Untitled, c. 1978
Graphite on paper
20 × 30 in.
ID #1128
Mary Ann Unger Estate

Untitled, 1978
Graphite on paper
22 × 30 in.
ID #1131
Mary Ann Unger Estate

Untitled, 1978
Etching with watercolor
and colored pencil
22½ × 30 in.
ID #1144
Mary Ann Unger Estate

Untitled, 1978
Etching with watercolor
22½ × 30 in.
ID #1147
Mary Ann Unger Estate

*Untitled (Study for
Hexagonal Quintet)*,
1978
Watercolor and pencil
on paper
20½ × 26¾ in.
ID #1151
Mary Ann Unger Estate
Fig. 1.19

Untitled, c. 1978
Graphite on paper
22½ × 30 in.
ID #1154
Mary Ann Unger Estate

Untitled, 1978
Colored pencil on paper
17 × 24 in.
ID #1254
Mary Ann Unger Estate

Untitled, 1978
Watercolor and
graphite on paper
6½ × 6½ in.
ID #1461
Mary Ann Unger Estate

Untitled, 1978
Watercolor on paper
6½ × 6 in.
ID #1462
Mary Ann Unger Estate

Untitled, 1978
Watercolor on paper
6½ × 6 in.
ID #1465
Mary Ann Unger Estate

Untitled, 1978
Watercolor on paper
6½ × 6 in.
ID #1468
Mary Ann Unger Estate

Untitled, 1978
Watercolor on paper
6½ × 6 in.
ID #1471
Mary Ann Unger Estate

Untitled, 1978
Watercolor on paper
6½ × 6 in.
ID #1472
Mary Ann Unger Estate

Untitled, 1978
Watercolor on paper
6½ × 6 in.
ID #1473
Mary Ann Unger Estate

Untitled, 1978
Watercolor and
graphite on paper
6½ × 4½ in.
ID #1475
Mary Ann Unger Estate

Untitled, 1978
Watercolor on paper
6½ × 6 in.
ID #1479
Mary Ann Unger Estate

Untitled, 1978
Watercolor and
graphite on paper
4 × 5 in.
ID #1528
Mary Ann Unger Estate

Untitled, 1978
Watercolor on paper
4½ × 8 in.
ID #1532
Mary Ann Unger Estate

Untitled (2 pieces), 1978
Watercolor on paper
Overall: 3½ × 6 in.
ID #1547
Mary Ann Unger Estate

Untitled, 1978
Watercolor on paper
2½ × 5 in.
ID #1549
Mary Ann Unger Estate

*Study for Across the
Bering Strait*, 1992
Graphite on paper
30 × 22¼ in.
ID #1080
Mary Ann Unger Estate

Untitled, 1992
Graphite on paper
30 × 22¼ in.
ID #1083
Mary Ann Unger Estate

Amazon Series V, 1994
Etching
18¾ × 24 in.
ID #1035
Mary Ann Unger Estate

Across the Bering Strait,
c. 1995
Graphite on paper
20 × 27½ in.
ID #1212
Mary Ann Unger Estate

Across the Bering Strait,
1995
Graphite on paper
17 × 22 in.
ID #1392
Mary Ann Unger Estate

*Across the Bering Strait
(Cut Out)*, 1995
Charcoal on paper
17 × 19 in.
ID #1393
Mary Ann Unger Estate

Spine, 1996
Graphite on paper
19 × 17½ in.
ID #1039
Mary Ann Unger Estate

Shades, Study 2, 1996
Charcoal on paper
22 × 17 in.
ID #1391
Mary Ann Unger Estate

Untitled, 1996
Watercolor on paper
12½ × 10 in.
ID #1410
Mary Ann Unger Estate

Untitled, c. 1996
Watercolor on paper
12½ × 9½ in.
ID #1430
Mary Ann Unger Estate
Fig. 1.21

Untitled, n.d.
12½ × 9½ in.
Watercolor on paper
ID #1431
Mary Ann Unger Estate

Across the Bering Strait,
1994
Graphite on paper
9 × 20 in.
ID #1659
Mary Ann Unger Estate

Untitled, n.d.
Acrylic on paper
12½ × 17½ in.
ID #1674
Mary Ann Unger Estate

Untitled, n.d.
Ink and graphite
on paper
18 × 12 in.
ID #1677
Mary Ann Unger Estate

Untitled, n.d.
Ink and graphite
on paper
18 × 12 in.
ID #1733
Mary Ann Unger Estate

Untitled, n.d.
Acrylic on paper
13 × 17 in.
ID #1735
Mary Ann Unger Estate

**Eve Biddle: Works
in Conversation**

*New Relics Expanded
Perspective*, 2019
Silkscreen on cotton
paper
22 × 30 in. (unframed)
Eve Biddle Studio

*New Relics Expanded
Perspective*, 2019
Silkscreen on cotton
paper
22 × 30 in. (unframed)
Eve Biddle Studio

New Relics, 2020
Ceramic with glaze
11 × 10½ × 1½ in.
Eve Biddle Studio

New Relics, 2021
Ceramic with glaze
22 × 6½ × 3 in.
Eve Biddle Studio

New Relics: Chain, 2021
Ceramic with glaze
22 × 22 × 22 in.
Eve Biddle Studio

New Relics: Trilobite,
2021
Ceramic with glaze
17 × 6 × 3½ in.
Eve Biddle Studio

All works collection of Williams College Museum of Art, arranged by date of acquisition or accession number

Maker(s) unknown;
Italian
South Italian lekythos,
550–250 BCE
Terracotta
6⅝ × 11⅛ in.
Gift of Mrs. John W.
Field, CG.12

Maker(s) unknown;
possibly Corinthian-
Greek
Corinthian aryballos,
650–550 BCE
Terracotta
4⁷⁄₁₆ × 9⅝ in.
Gift of Mrs. John W.
Field, CG.34

Maker(s) unknown;
Italian
Oinochoë with cover,
450–200 BCE
Terracotta
5¹¹⁄₁₆ × 16¹⁵⁄₁₆ in.
Gift of Mrs. John W.
Field, CG.35

Maker(s) unknown;
Italian
Gnathia ware oinochoë,
450–200 BCE
Terracotta
9³⁄₁₆ × 15¹¹⁄₁₆ in.
Gift of Mrs. John W.
Field, CG.37

Maker(s) unknown;
Peruvian(?)
Stirrup-spout bottle,
1–500 CE
Clay
9¼ × 17⁷⁄₁₆ in.
Gift of Mrs. John W.
Field, 1887.1.33

Maker(s) unknown;
Greek
Pyxis with lid, n.d.
Terracotta
3¼ × 2⁷⁄₁₆ in.
Gift of Mrs. John W.
Field, 1887.1.44

Maker(s) unknown;
Etruscan
Lekythos, n.d.
Terracotta, bucchero
ware
4⅝ × 8⅞ in.
Gift of Mrs. John W. Field
1887.1.50

Maker(s) unknown;
believed Pueblo
Bowl with triangular
designs, c. 1300–1700 CE
Clay
4⁵⁄₁₆ in. (circumference);
3⁷⁄₁₆ in. (rim)
Gift of Edmund
Seymour, Class of 1882,
30.2.5

Maker(s) unknown;
Italian
Cart decoration, "Virgin
in Glory," n.d.
Painted wood
6⁷⁄₁₆ × 7³⁄₁₆ × 2¼ in.
Bequest of Karl E.
Weston, Class of 1896,
56.16.4.D

Maker(s) unknown;
Spanish(?)
Standing Virgin, c. 16th
century
Polychrome and gilding
on wood
11¹³⁄₁₆ in. (height); 3¹⁄₁₆ in.
(base)
Bequest of Karl E.
Weston, Class of 1896,
56.16.17

Maker(s) unknown;
Egyptian
Statuette of Isis nursing
infant Horus
(Harpokrates), late
Ptolemaic–Early Roman
period (100 BCE–200 CE)
Bronze
5¾ × 1¼ in.
Gift of Horace Mayer,
59.21.18

Maker(s) unknown;
Egyptian
Shawabti of Iset-m-
kheb, daughter of
Paynozem, c. 1000 BCE
Faience
Dimensions unrecorded
Gift of Horace Mayer,
61.19.6

Helen Pashgian, b. 1934
Untitled, 1969
Cast epoxy on metal
base
9⁷⁄₁₆ × 12 × 18⅞ in.
Gift of Susan W. and
Stephen D. Paine, Class
of 1954, 74.45

Ibram Lassaw,
1913–2003
Untitled, 1970
Welded bronze and
steel
14⅜ × 12⅝ × 8⅞ in.
Gift of Sam Hunter, Class
of 1944, 75.34

Herbert Ferber,
1906–1991
*Maquette for Wall
Sculpture*, 1952–53
Copper and lead on
painted-wood backing
12½ × 9 × 1½ in.
Bequest of Lawrence H.
Bloedel, Class of 1923,
77.9.35

Toshio Odate, b. 1930
Geisha, 1962
Wood (London plane
tree)
67 × 17¾ × 16 in.
Bequest of Lawrence H.
Bloedel, Class of 1923,
77.9.71

Louise Nevelson,
1899–1988
Sky Wave, 1964
Painted wood with
metal hardware
94 × 48 × 14½ in.
Bequest of Lawrence H.
Bloedel, Class of 1923,
77.9.108

Kongo; present-day
Democratic Republic of
the Congo
N'kisi, c. 19th–20th
century
Wood and various
media
11 × 4¼ × 3 in.
Museum purchase,
Karl E. Weston Memorial
Fund, 77.22

Maker(s) unknown;
possibly Boeotian-
Greek
Standing goddess,
c. 600–550 BCE
Polychromed terracotta
6⁵⁄₁₆ × 2¾ in.
Gift of the son and
daughters of Charles
Bolles-Rogers, Class of
1907: Frederick Van D.
Rogers, Mary Rogers
Savage, and Nancy
Rogers Pierson, 77.63.33

Robert Janz, b. 1932
3 Cherry Planes: Any Arrangement, 1978
Wood (cherrywood case inserted with two removable wood slats)
11⅝ × ½ × 1⁵⁄₁₆ in.
Museum purchase, Joseph O. Eaton Fund, Greylock Foundation, Charles Webb Fund, 79.13.A

Maker(s) unknown; French
Madonna, 18th century
Gilt bronze
5¹³⁄₁₆ × 3⅞ × 1⅞ in.
Gift of John Davis Hatch V, in memory of Baroness Halkett, 79.19.2

Bessie Potter Vonnoh, 1872–1955
Mother Nursing Child, 1902
Bronze
7⅜ × 5⅝ × 6⁵⁄₁₆ in.
Gift of Lois Clarke, 79.32

The Kalaallit People, East Greenland
Kayak model with figure, c. 1945
Leather, bone, and wood
18⅞ × 1¾ × 3¾ in.
Gift of Susan W. and Stephen D. Paine, Class of 1954, 81.45.7

Rendille Cultural Group, present-day Kenya
Neckrest and stool combination, 19th–20th century
Wood
9⅝ × 11¼ × 6⅛ in.
Museum purchase, John B. Turner '24 Memorial Fund, 84.13.15

Maker(s) unknown; Portuguese colonial settlement in the Americas or India
Madonna and Child, 17th century
Ivory
14⁵⁄₁₆ × 5¼ × 4⁷⁄₁₆ in.
Museum purchase, Karl E. Weston Memorial Fund, 84.22

Dimitri Hadzi, 1921–2006
Maquette, n.d.
Bronze
7½ in. (height)
Bequest of Jane T. Ritchie, 85.24.34.A

Dimitri Hadzi, 1921–2006
Abstract, n.d.
Bronze on stone base
8¾ × 10¼ in.
Bequest of Jane T. Ritchie, 85.24.36

Eduardo Luigi Paolozzi, 1924–2005
Untitled, n.d.
Bronze
10¼ × 4 × 3¼ in.
Bequest of Jane T. Ritchie, 85.24.42

Robert Adams, 1917–1984
Maquette for Ovoid Variation No. 1, 1980
Cast bronze
5⅜ × 5½ × ½ in.
Bequest of Jane T. Ritchie, 85.46.41

Akamba or Boran Cultural Group; present-day Kenya
Lukoso (armlet), c. 19th–20th century
Ivory
5¼ × 1¹⁄₁₆ in.
Gift of Ernie Wolfe III, Class of 1972, 85.47.9

George Warren Rickey, 1907–2002
Sedge #5, 1962
Stainless steel on wood base
19⁵⁄₁₆ × 5⅛ × 3¹⁵⁄₁₆ in.
Bequest of Professor Donald and Mary Richmond, 87.22.1

Dimitri Hadzi, 1921–2006
Maquette, n.d.
Bronze
7⅜ in. (height)
Bequest of Jane T. Ritchie, 85.24.34.C

Claire Falkenstein, 1908–1997
A Glass Ball, 1972
Venetian blown glass
8 × 8 in.
Gift of Peggie Dwight, 90.40.12

Makonde Cultural Group; present-day Tanzania and Mozambique
Mask, 19th–20th century
Wood
18 × 6 × 4⅛ in.
Donor unrecorded, 1993, 93.1.4

The Maya Civilization, present-day Mexico
Jade beads, 600–900 CE
Worked jade
5⅛ in.
Donor unrecorded, 1993, 93.1.16.B

Maker(s) unknown
Vessel, n.d.
Gourd
2¹⁄₁₆ in. (rim)
Donor unrecorded, 93.1.65.A

Maker(s) unknown
Fragment from a mosaic, n.d.
Stone mosaic set in cement
4⅛ × 4⅜ in.
Anonymous gift, 93.1.114

Maker(s) unknown
Fragment from a mosaic, n.d.
Stone mosaic
2³⁄₁₆ × 2³⁄₁₆ in.
Anonymous gift, 93.1.115

Maker(s) unknown
[Tool], n.d.
Stone
9⁷⁄₁₆ × 2³⁄₁₆ in.
Anonymous gift, 93.1.130.E

Maker(s) unknown
Axe head, n.d.
Stone
6⁷⁄₁₆ × 4¹⁄₁₆ × 1½ in.
Anonymous gift, 93.1.130.G

Maker(s) unknown
Axe head, n.d.
Stone
6¹⁵⁄₁₆ × 2⁹⁄₁₆ × 1¹⁄₁₆ in.
Anonymous gift, 93.1.130.H

Louise Nevelson, 1899–1988
Sun-set, 1981
Painted wood
12½ × 18 × 2¾ in.
Gift of Michael Dively, Class of 1961, 94.2.2

Louise Bourgeois, 1911–2010
Nature Study #3, 1985; cast 1987
Bronze with patina
11 × 18 × 13 in.
Museum purchase, Kathryn Hurd Fund, 96.1

Yoruba Cultural Group;
present-day Nigeria
Shango dance wand
(*ose Sango*), 20th
century
Wood, beads, pigment,
patina
12⅝ × 3½ × 2⅞ in.
Gift of Dr. Oliver E. and
Pamela F. Cobb, Class of
1952, M.2002.3.1

Kongo; present-day
Democratic Republic of
the Congo
N'kisi, 20th century
Wood, mixed media
13¼ × 5 × 3¾ in.
Gift of Dr. Oliver E. and
Pamela F. Cobb, Class of
1952, M.2002.3.6

Louise Bourgeois,
1911–2010
*EYES, Model for 75th
Anniversary sculpture
commission Eyes*, 2000
Plaster
4 × 7 × 6¾ in.
Gift of the artist,
M.2002.14.A

Hans Arp, 1886–1966
Lunar Armor, 1938
Granite
10¹¹⁄₁₆ × 18⅛ × 12⅜ in.
Temporary loan from
the Collection of the
Sally and Eliot Robinson
Family, TL.2003.103.2

Hans Arp, 1886–1966
*Couronne de Bourgeons
I*, 1936; cast 1959
Bronze
18½ × 15 × 9 in.
Gift of Sylvia and Joseph
Slifka, M.2004.4.1

David Hammons,
b. 1943
Rock Fan, 1997
Fabric mounted on
paper affixed to stone
12 × 18 × 17 in.
Museum purchase,
Kathryn Hurd Fund,
M.2004.10

Kuba Cultural Group;
present-day
Democratic Republic of
the Congo
Headrest, 19th or 20th
century
Wood
6½ × 21 × 3 in.
Gift of Dr. Oliver E. and
Pamela F. Cobb, Class of
1952, M.2011.21.2

Katy Schimert, b. 1963
*Untitled (Porcelain
Stone)*, 1995–97
*Untitled (Porcelain
Stone)*, 1995–97
*Untitled (Porcelain
Stone)*, 1995–97
Waxed slip-cast
porcelain
Each: 8 × 10 × 10 in.
Gift of Peter Norton,
M.2015.17.52; M.2015.17.
53; M.2015.17.54

Beverly Semmes,
b. 1958
Pot #12, 1994
Satin-glazed ceramic
19 × 5¾ × 3 in.
Gift of Peter Norton,
M.2015.17.55

Beverly Semmes,
b. 1958
Pot #11, 1994
Satin-glazed ceramic
8 × 6 × 3 in.
Gift of Peter Norton,
M.2015.17.56

Maren Hassinger,
b. 1947
Maquette for Walking,
c. 1978
Wire
15 × 6 × 7 in.
Gift of Peter Hassinger,
Class of 1967, M.2017.16

Yoruba Cultural Group;
present-day Nigeria
Basket with female
head stopper, c. early
20th century
Wood, dyed woven fiber
Stopper: 4¾ × 3½ in.
Container: 7 × 7½ in.
Gift of Drs. Carolyn and
Eli Newberger,
M.2017.17.8

The Fante Cultural
Group; present-day
Ghana
Fertility figure,
c. 19th–20th century
Wood
12³⁄₁₆ × 3⅛ × 3⅛ in.
Gift of Scott Alan Krol,
WCMA Reserve
Collection, RC.6.2

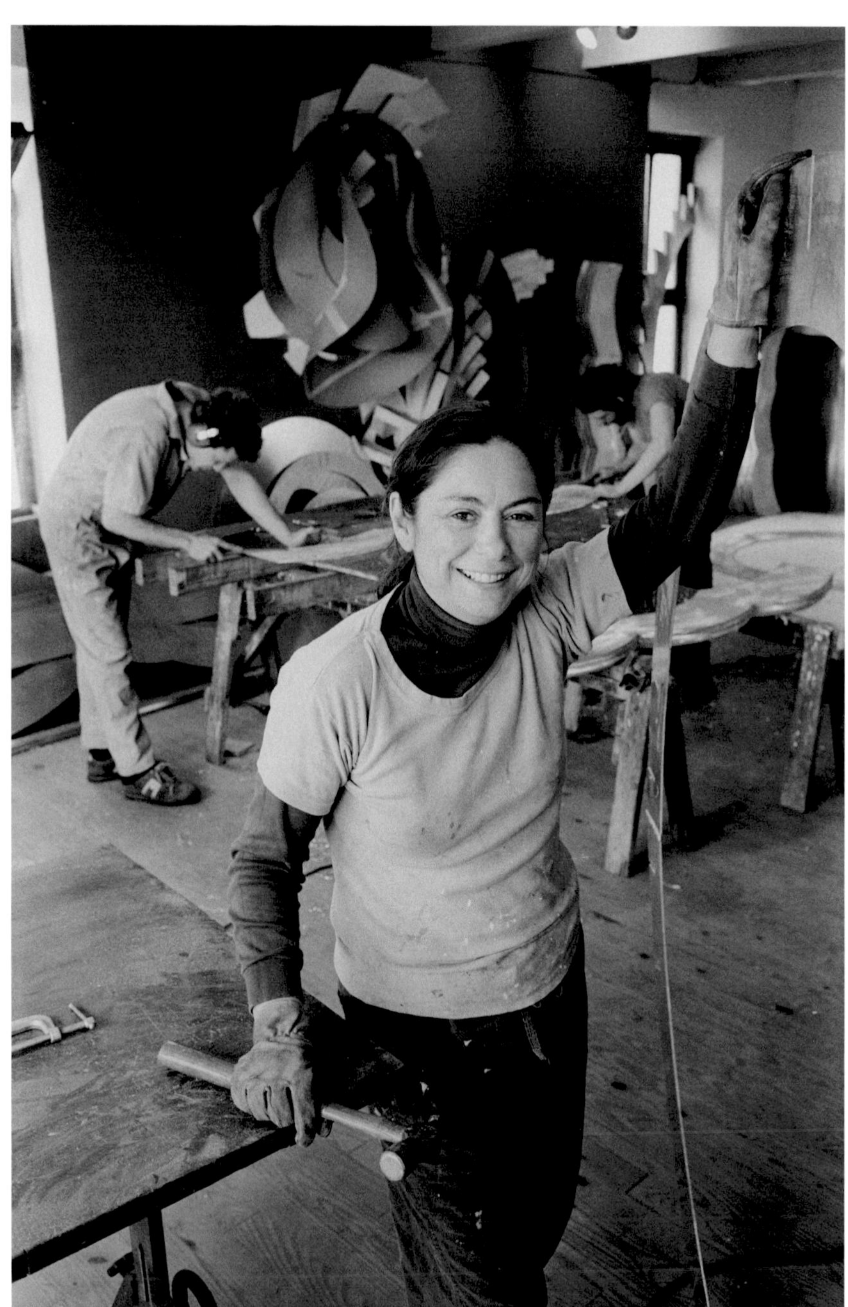

Mary Ann Unger, 53, a Noted Sculptor and Curator, Is Dead

Roberta Smith

Reprinted from the
New York Times,
January 3, 1999

Mary Ann Unger, a sculptor and curator, died on Monday at her home in Manhattan. She was 53.

The cause was breast cancer, her family said.

Born in New York in 1945, Ms. Unger began making sculpture as a child in art classes at the Museum of Modern Art. In 1967, she received a bachelor's degree in art at Mount Holyoke College, where she learned to weld, cast bronze and carve marble. After a year of graduate school at the University of California at Berkeley, she spent several years traveling, including a trip alone through North Africa. She then received a master of fine arts degree in 1975 from Columbia University, where she studied with Ronald Bladen and George Sugarman. The playful, undulating shapes of the pieces she started exhibiting in the late 1970s reflected Mr. Sugarman's influence.

These evolved into tensile structures whose repeating arcs evoked both Islamic architecture and boughs of trees. The style served Ms. Unger well in numerous public commissions, most recently in 1991 with *Ode to Tatlin*, a pair of tall, crisp colonnadelike curving forms that face each other, forming a kind of elliptical gateway, at the Aaron Copland School of Music at Queens College.

After Ms. Unger's breast cancer was diagnosed in 1985, she exhibited a more expressionistic side in her art. Over the next several years she became known for dark, bulbous, beamlike forms that she often laid out or propped up in clusters. Made of Hydrocal, a lightweight plaster, over steel armatures, with surfaces that appeared to be scarred and scorched, these pieces could suggest giant twigs, human limbs or sausages, as well as the aftermath of some mysterious ritual or catastrophe.

In their effort to conjure the body without actually depicting it, these works occupied a territory defined by Eva Hesse and Louise Bourgeois. But the pieces combined a sense of mythic power with a sensitivity to shape that was all their own, achieving a subtlety of expression that belied their monumental scale.

Ms. Unger's work is in the collections of the Hirschhorn Museum and Sculpture Garden in Washington, the Brooklyn Museum of Art and the Philadelphia Museum of Art. Her most recent solo show was at the Trans Hudson Gallery on West 13th Street in Manhattan in 1997. She had recently completed a series of works that are to be shown at Trans Hudson in May.

She is survived by her husband, Geoffrey Biddle, a photographer and assistant chairman of photography at the Parsons School of Design; a daughter, Eve; her parents, William and Dorothy Unger of Tenafly, NJ, and a brother, Christopher Unger of Milwaukee.

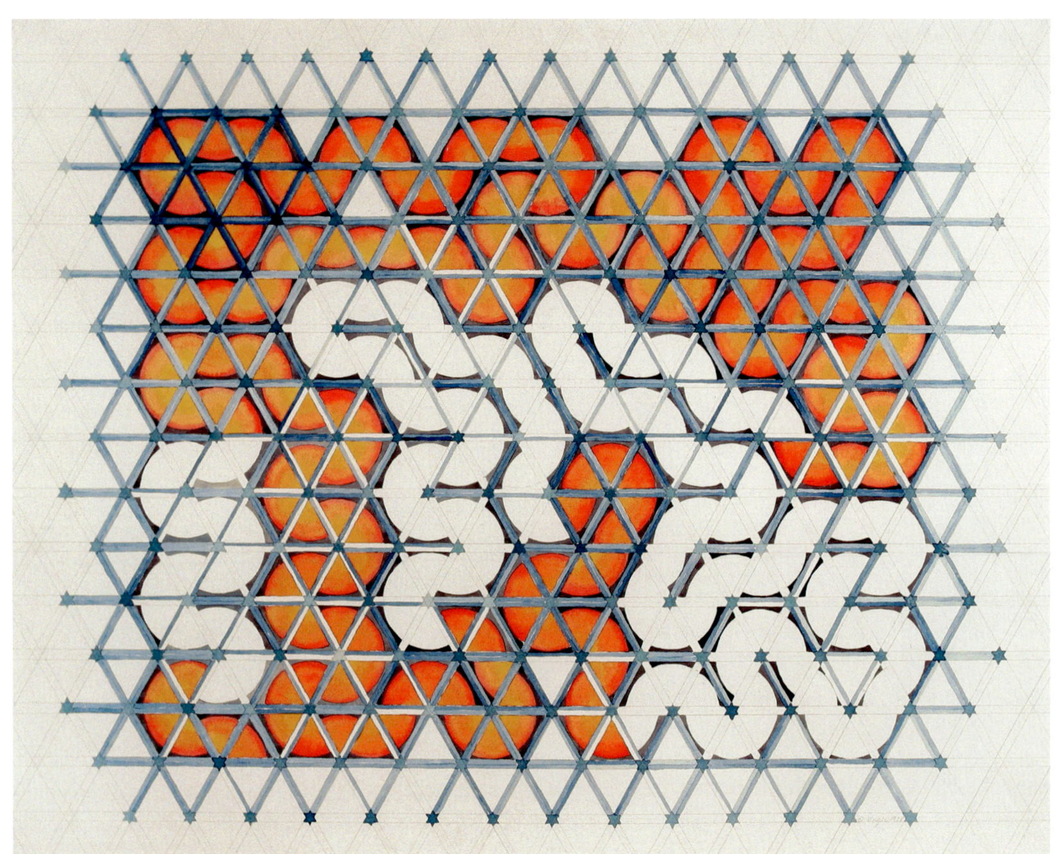

Further Reading + Research/Works Cited

Mary Ann Unger Estate
5 E. Third Street, New York, NY 10003
www.maryannunger.com

Artist Talks

Biddle, Eve, moderator, with Brooke Kamin
Rappaport, Douglas Dreishpoon, and
Petah Coyne. "Mary Ann Unger Talk."
February 10, 2016. http://vimeo
.com/160037295/489fb41875.

Meadmore, Clement, moderator, with John L.
Moore, Robert Murray, Peter Stroud,
Martin Bull, and Mary Ann Unger. "Abstrac-
tion as a Timeless Art Form." Artists Talk
on Art. Fulcrum Gallery, SoHo, New York,
January 21, 1994. Artists Talk on Art
Records, circa 1974–2018. Archives of
American Art, Smithsonian Institution.

Woodman, George, moderator, with Gloria
Klein, Tony Robbin, Mary Ann Unger,
Charles DiJulio, Richard Kallweit, and Clark
Richert. "Systematic/Metrical Patterning:
In-Town and Out-of-Town." Artists Talk on
Art. January 11, 1980. Artists Talk on Art
Records, circa 1974–2018. Archives of
American Art, Smithsonian Institution.

Contexts

Beasley, Sara C. "Leonard DeLonga: Artist-
Teacher-Bodhisattva." *Buddhistdoor
Global*, March, 10, 2020.

Brenson, Michael. "Jasper Johns Prints on
Show at the Modern." *New York Times*,
May 23, 1986.

Gaines, Charles. "Negotiating Abstraction."
In *Howardena Pindell: What Remains to
Be Seen*, edited by Naomi Beckwith and
Valerie Cassel Oliver. New York: Prestel,
2018. Published online, http://pindell
.mcachicago.org/essays/howardena
-pindell-negotiating-abstraction/.

Johnson, Ken. "A Romantic Pushes Minimalism to the Maximum," *New York Times*,
February 19, 1999.

Kimmelman, Michael. "Review/Art: Sculpture,
Sculpture Everywhere." *New York Times*,
July 31, 1992.

Larson, Kay. "Small Wonders." *New York
Magazine*, March 30, 1992.

Lippard, Lucy. "Eccentric Abstraction." In
Changing: Essays in Art Criticism. New
York: E. P. Dutton, 1971.

Lowery, Rebecca Skafsgaard. "Criss-Cross and
the Gender of Pattern-Making." In *With
Pleasure: Pattern and Decoration in
American Art: 1972–1985*, edited by Ann
Lowery. New Haven, CT: Yale University
Press, 2019.

Pan, Shannon Collins. *DeLonga: A Mini Collection. A Pictorial Look at the Art of Leonard DeLonga*. Blurb Books, 2009.

Pincus-Witten, Robert. *Postminimalism into Maximalism: American Art, 1966–1986*. Ann Arbor: UMI Research Press, 1986.

Pollock, Griselda. "Encountering Encounter: An Introduction." In *Encountering Eva Hesse*, edited by Griselda Pollock and Vanessa Corby. New York: Prestel, 2006.

Ridge, Emily. "Introduction." In *Portable Modernisms: The Art of Traveling Light*. Edinburgh: Edinburgh University Press, 2017.

Russell, John. "Art That Tells of the Jewish Experience." *New York Times*, October 24, 1975.

Smith, Roberta. "George Sugarman, a Sculptor of Colorful Works, Dies at 87." Obituary, *New York Times*, August 31, 1999.

Smith, Roberta. "Mary Ann Unger, 53, a Noted Sculptor and Curator, Is Dead." Obituary, *New York Times*, January 3, 1999.

Smith, Roberta. "Minoru Niizuma, 67, Sculptor and Teacher." Obituary, *New York Times*, September 29, 1998.

Harthorn, Sandy, and Kathleen Bettis. *Fabricated Nature*. Boise: Boise Art Museum, 1994.

Hill, Jen. *White Horizon: The Arctic in the Nineteenth-Century British Imagination*. Albany: SUNY Press, 2008.

Laughlin, W. S. "Human Migration and Permanent Occupation in the Bering Sea Area." In *The Bering Land Bridge*, edited by David Moody Hopkins. Stanford, CA: Stanford University Press, 1967.

Le Guin, Ursula K. *The Carrier Bag Theory of Fiction*. New York: Ignota, 2019.

Müller-Beck, Hansjürgen. "On Migrations of Hunters across the Bering Land Bridge in the Upper Pleistocene." In *The Bering Land Bridge*, edited by David Moody Hopkins. Stanford, CA: Stanford University Press, 1967.

Scarry, Elaine. *The Body in Pain: The Making and Unmaking of the World*. New York: Oxford University Press, 1985.

Vaughn, Sue Fisher. "The Female Hero in Science Fiction and Fantasy: 'Carrier-Bag' to 'No-Road.'" *Journal of the Fantastic in the Arts* 4, no. 4 (1991): 83–96.

Human Histories

Edwards, Lee R. "The Labors of Psyche: Toward a Theory of Female Heroism." *Critical Inquiry* 6, no. 1 (Autumn 1979): 33–49.

Farb, Peter. *Man's Rise to Civilization as Shown by the Indians of North America from Primeval Times to the Coming of the Industrial State*. New York: E. P. Dutton, 1968.

Fillippone, Christine. *Science, Technology, and Utopias: Women Artists and Cold War America*. New York: Routledge, 2019.

Fisher, Elizabeth. *Woman's Creation: Sexual Evolution and the Shaping of Society*. New York: McGraw-Hill, 1980.

Haag, William G. "The Bering Strait Land Bridge." *Scientific American* 206, no. 1 (January 1962), http://www.scientificamerican.com/article/the-bering-strait-land-bridge/.

Sculpture: History + Specific Practices

Andersen, Wayne. *American Sculpture in Process, 1930–1970*. Boston: New York Graphic Society, 1975.

Asawa, Ruth. Cited in, "The Art of Space: Ruth Asawa's Sculptural Installations." In *The Sculpture of Ruth Asawa: Contours in the Air*, edited by Timothy Anglin Burgland and Daniel Cornell. Berkeley: University of California Press, 2006.

Bal, Mieke. "Autotopography: Louise Bourgeois as Builder." *Biography* 25, no. 1 (Winter 2002), http://www.jstor.org/stable/23540717.

Benezra, Neal, and Olga M. Viso. *Distemper: Dissonant Themes in the Art of the 1990s*. Washington, DC: Hirshhorn Museum and Sculpture Garden, Smithsonian Institution, 1996.

Birkhofer, Denise. "Eva Hesse and Mira Schendel: Voiding the Body—Embodying the Void." *Woman's Art Journal* 31, no. 2

(Fall/Winter 2010), http://www.jstor.org
/stable/41331079.

Carson, Fiona. "Sculpture and Installation." In *Feminist Visual Culture*, by Fiona Carson and Claire Pajaczkowksa. Edinburgh: Edinburgh University Press, 2000.

Chave, Anna C. "Sculpture, Gender, and the Value of Labor." *American Art* 24, no. 1 (Spring 2010), http://www.journals .uchicago.edu/doi/abs/10.1086/652740.

Fer, Briony. "Objects Beyond Objecthood." *Oxford Art Journal* 22, no. 2 (1999): 25–36.

Hepworth, Barbara. *Barbara Hepworth: Carvings and Drawings*, with an introduction by Herbert Read. London: Lund Humphries, 1952.

Hepworth, Barbara. *Unit 1: The Modern Movement in English Architecture, Painting and Sculpture*, edited by Herbert Read. London: Cassell, 1934.

Hodin, J. P. *Barbara Hepworth*. New York: David McKay, 1961.

Kampf, Avram. *Luise Kaish: Sculpture*. New York: Jewish Museum, 1973.

Krauss, Rosalind. "The Double Negative: A New Syntax for Sculpture." In *New Passages for Sculpture*, 243–77. Cambridge, MA: MIT Press, 1977.

Krauss, Rosalind. "Louise Bourgeois: Portrait of the Artist as Fillete." In *Bachelors*, 51–74. Cambridge, MA: MIT Press, 1999.

Krauss, Rosalind. *Perpetual Inventory*. Cambridge, MA: MIT Press, 2010.

Krauss, Rosalind. "Sculpture in the Expanded Field." *October* 8 (Spring 1979): 30–44.

Kross, Margaret. "Openings: ektor garcia." *Artforum*, September 2019. http://www .artforum.com/print/201907/margaret -kross-on-ektor-garcia-80524.

Sharp, Sarah Rose. "Sanford Biggers at MOCAD." *Detroit Art Review*, September 13, 2016.

Curatorial Acknowledgements

In the summer 1980 issue of *Art Journal*, the influential art critic Lawrence Alloway published a scathing critique of men and museums in the New York art world. Alloway challenged the Museum of Modern Art to organize an exhibition provocatively titled *Post-Masculine Art: Women Artists, 1970–1980*, meant to be "a timely corrective," Alloway jabbed, to "NY's curatorial chauvinism" (295).

Alloway asserted that the show's guest curator must be masc-identified in order for the art world to take notice, and volunteered himself. He then proposed a veritable who's-who of female essayists and scholars who might contribute to the catalogue (those "capable of carrying the subject… beyond the primitive level of present discussions"). Curiously, Alloway offered no checklist and never named or pointed to specific artists. He articulated his aesthetic and curatorial sensibilities by stating that the works on view would "cover representational painting, abstract art (including pattern painting), Process art, Conceptual art, outdoor and indoor sculpture (the latter including fiber works), video art, and performance" (read: the capacious genres covered by MoMA's exhibition and education program in the previous year that could have easily featured female artists, but did not).

Though not named in the text, a photograph of Mary Ann Unger's iron-form work *Benchmarks* (1977) concludes the satirical project proposal as a paratext, a kind of knuckled metaphor. The abstracted tubular elements, jointed at a bulbous expansion like two legs crossed, form a fitting—and pointed—end. A "benchmark" indeed. And while Unger had already featured in a brief 1977 MoMA PS1 exhibition (*10 Downtown: 10 Years*), her work still has yet to take its rightful place center stage in an exhibition at the Modern, let alone be acquired for the museum's collection. More than forty years on, Alloway's photographic allusion connotes a benchmark in diversity, inclusivity, parity, and presence that the art world has yet to achieve.

One assumes the ongoing oversight—after Alloway so forcibly instrumentalized Unger in his dated but appreciatively inclusive critique of the art world—stems as much from the deep-seated phallocentric histories of Minimalism in the Americas as it does from Unger's expansive crisscrossing of genres, which inhibits easy categorization. The "masculinist mode" of Alloway's ire has much in common with the conceptual desire to be without history. To be *au fond*, current, now. Unger's practice, by contrast, *revels* in history—her own, that of her ancestors, that of all peoples.

Mary Ann Unger: To Shape a Moon from Bone positions Unger and her practice within and against the male-dominated milieu of which Alloway wrote. In giving close attention to the formal preoccupations and trajectories of Unger's training and practice, the exhibition and its catalogue offer an understanding of the ways in which Unger was at the forefront of expressive typographies of sculpture in the early decades of postmodern art.

I first encountered the work and legacy of Mary Ann Unger on a mild Thursday morning in April 2018. At the invitation of Eve Biddle, I traveled by train along the Hudson at sunrise to the city, took a cab from Penn Station, walked up eight stories, and came into a large space. I have been trying to find the words to convey the impressive power and the historical resonance of what I saw, and how I felt, since that first encounter. During the anxious days of the global pandemic, Unger was my muse. Her curiosity and unflappable spirit gave me hope. I am indebted to her and the world she gave me.

I am likewise indebted to Eve Biddle, Geoffrey Biddle, Josh Frankel, and Allison Kaufman for their love and their trust in me to steward such an important project for Unger's legacy and for the field of modern American art.

I am grateful for Mary Davidson, Max Davidson III, Max Davidson IV, Charles Davidson, Brittany LoSchiavo, and other dear friends at the Davidson Gallery for their excitement for the project, their collective and continual generosity to me, and their deep love of Williams College and of the Williams College Museum of Art.

I am in awe of the creativity and research skills of Zoe Dobuler MA '21, whose essay opens original, transdisciplinary ground on Unger's practice. I am still in a state of delighted disbelief that Sarah Montross, Associate Curator at deCordova Sculpture Park and Museum, made such generous time to engage with the project.

Jonathan Odden MA '20, and Ben Ward BA '22, served as curatorial research interns on the project. Their hunting through digitized and undigitized archives and their synthesis of disparate articles and yearbook data into careful lists and spreadsheets during a global pandemic was nothing short of miraculous.

Andrée Heller's and Julie Reiter's early excitement for the project helped translate a big idea into an exhibition proposal that centered Unger's voice. Thank you. The shape of the project, especially the attentions of the catalogue, owes much to conversations with Michelle Apotsos and Lisa Dorin at Williams College; Anne Thompson, Suzanne Lemberg Usdan Gallery at Bennington College; Robert Wiesenberger, Sterling and Francine Clark Art Institute; Reto Thüring, Museum of Fine Arts, Boston; Stephanie Sparling-Williams, Mount Holyoke College Art Museum; Emma Chubb, Smith College Museum of Art; and Jane Panetta, Whitney Museum of American Art, respectively.

When this exhibition opens in summer 2022, I will have transitioned to a new role at a new institution. While my new colleagues eagerly anticipate the show, it is right to end my acknowledgements by thanking the people who allowed the idea to take root in their minds and on their calendars, and whose collective care brought the project to its fullest flower. My colleagues at the Williams College Museum of Art are miraculous. In the ways this project succeeds, it is their triumph. Its weak moments are my singular failing. I dedicate this to them, for they have taught me, by example, the extraordinary potential of academic museums.

Horace D. Ballard, Theodore E. Stebbins Associate Curator of American Art, Harvard Art Museums; former Curator of American Art, Williams College Museum of Art

Published in conjunction with the exhibition
Mary Ann Unger: To Shape a Moon from Bone, curated
by Horace D. Ballard, on view at the Williams College
Museum of Art, July–December 2022.

Library of Congress Cataloging-in-Publication Data

Names: Ballard, Horace D., editor. | Franks, Pamela,
    writer of foreword.
Title: Mary Ann Unger : to shape a moon from bone /
    edited by Horace D. Ballard ; with contributions
    from Eve Biddle, Zoe Dobuler, and Sarah Montross.
Description: Williamstown, Massachusetts : Williams
    College Museum of Art, [2022] | Includes
    bibliographical references.
Identifiers: LCCN 2021062559 | ISBN 9781646570263
    (hardcover)
Subjects: LCSH: Unger, Mary Ann--Exhibitions.
Classification: LCC NB237.U53 A4 2022 | DDC 730.92--
    dc23/eng/20220301
LC record available at https://lccn.loc.gov/2021062559

Published by
Williams College Museum of Art
15 Lawrence Hall Drive, Suite 2
Williamstown, MA 01267
wcma.williams.edu

Distributed by
ARTBOOK|D.A.P.
75 Broad Street, Suite 630
New York, NY 10004
artbook.com

Produced by
Lucia|Marquand, Seattle
luciamarquand.com

Edited by Kristin Swan
Designed by Ryan Polich
Typeset in Utile and American Typewriter by
    Tina Henderson
Proofread by Carrie Wicks
Color management by I/O Color, Seattle
Printed and bound in China by Artron Art Group